The Melting Pot

OTHER BOOKS BY WALTER LAMP

The Decline and [Preventable] Fall of America
    ISBN 978-0-9834954-5-4   433 pages   ©2014

Offshore Plundering by American Companies
    ISBN 978-0-9834954-4-4   102 pages   ©2013

Biblical Verses, A Frank Study of the Old Testament
    and Hebrew Bible ISBN 978-0-9834954-2-0
                                            216 pages   ©2012

Koranic Verses, A Frank Study of the Koran
    ISBN 978-0-9816681-2-3   298 pages   ©2009

TAMAR, First Author of the Bible   2nd Edition
    ISBN 978-0-9816681-4-7   193 pages   ©2009

99 Prescriptions for a More Ethical Society
    ISBN 978-0-9816681-1-6   209 pages   ©2008

The Melting Pot

By Walter Lamp

RunningLight Publishing Company
Reno, Nevada

Lamp, Walter
The Melting Pot   /Walter Lamp   1st Edition

United States
Melting Pot / Assimilation / Immigration / Separatism
Differentiation / Multiculturalism / Diversity / History
Equality / Racism / Ghettos / Education / Socialism
Communism / Capitalism / Economic Inequality

ISBN 978-0-9834954-6-8

Library of Congress Control Number: 2019902476

Printed in the United States of America   10 9 8 7 6 5 4 3 2 1

Dedicated to my parents.

Table of Contents

THE MELTING POT

Introduction

I write *The Melting Pot* as a first generation American forever grateful for the play of the same title written by Israel Zangwill, a British national, which opened in Washington DC in 1908. I knew nothing of the play until recently, but I got to hear of the term "Melting Pot" and understand what it stood for decades ago. As a child of immigrants, raised in a virtual slum in Brooklyn NY and not even knowing I was deprived, I am here today and privileged to write this book.

Immigrants like my parents who were thankful for being accepted as Americans exemplify the Melting Pot, which concept was very popular concept back then. But it faded away in my generation as multiculturalism claimed the center stage. Today, the Melting Pot is hardly heard of and certainly not known by America's youth.

I recently became concerned with the never-ending controversy over immigration and with some multiculturists advocating deliberate maximization of cultural differences and the separation of cultures so that they don't melt with what they call mainstream America.

I remembered Abraham Lincoln had said "A house divided against itself cannot stand" and began to fear that America was heading that way. Hence the book, written with the hope of reminding us of the Melting Pot, introducing it to America's youth, and opposing too much separation in America.

1

THE MELTING POT

The Melting Pot

In the play entitled *"The Melting Pot"* that opened in Washington DC in 1908, an immigrant named David introduces the term "Melting-Pot" in the play's most salient and memorable declaration:

> "… America is God's Crucible, the great Melting-Pot where all the races of Europe are melting and re-forming! Here you stand, good folk, think I, when I see them at Ellis Island, here you stand in your fifty groups, with your fifty languages and histories, and your fifty blood hatreds and rivalries. But you won't be long like that, brothers, for these are the fires of God you've come to—these are the fires of God. A fig for your feuds and vendettas! Germans and Frenchmen, Irishmen and Englishmen, Jews and Russians—into the Crucible with you all! God is making the American."

David had been born in a pogrom-driven Russia and eventually migrated to America. The play dealt with immigrants coming to America and their assimilation into mainstream American society, but also devoted space to rant against the "freak-fashionables." Although the play was about "race" as it defined that term, the play had a philosophical bent with bigger than life characters.

The play was dedicated to President Theodore Roosevelt. He attended the opening performance in 1908. A year later the play moved to New York and the phrase "Melting Pot" quickly came into common use.

The author of the play was Israel Zangwill (1864-1926) a British national of the Jewish religion (the Jewish "race" according to the play). He had abandoned Zionism to become an advocate for mere emigration from oppressive lands, instead of pursuing the establishment of a Jewish homeland, by the time he wrote the play.

As terminology might cause confusion, as with the Melting Pot's use of the term "race," a brief examination of some common terms might be useful.

Ethnicity refers a geographic connection with an area or country and its common cultural traits.

Cultural traits can consist of common things or attributes, like language, faith or religion, mannerisms, diet, foods, entertainments, pastimes and much more that contribute to a way of life that make up a culture.

Heritage refers to the family, to your ancestors; who they were and where they came from. It doesn't refer to a person's current nationality as the ancestors could have come from another place. And it doesn't necessarily refer to a person's ethnicity as the person might never have been exposed to any of the ancestral cultural traits.

Nationality refers to the nation where the person was born, hold citizenship or resides. Some people were born or reside in areas that are not technically nations, but consider those areas as their nationality.

Race is usually based on physical characterizes, such as skin color, bone structure or eye shape or color. But this usage could vary as with the Melting Pot where it referred to ethnicity as identified by the common cultural traits found in a nation or faith/religion.

Assimilation

A whole chapter will be devoted to explaining assimilation; what it means, how it is accomplished, and where it leads.

For present purposes, just note that the Melting Pot assumes that immigrants will assimilate into, in the sense of joining, mainstream American society. The stated purpose of the Melting Pot crucible is to make Americans. Assimilation can be viewed as the process used to turn immigrants into Americans. And it obviously worked over the centuries before America even had a label for it. The label is assimilation, becoming one people in the new land.

Moving Away from the Melting Pot

An "I am an American" song was written for the 1939 New York World's Fair. This was, followed by the U.S. Immigration and Naturalization Service producing an "I Am an American" short film starring Humphrey Bogart and Danny Kaye and Congress declaring a day for observation in 1944. The phraseology suggests a connection with Melting Pot philosophy, but this didn't last long.

By 1952, Congress had renamed the day "Constitution Day" and finally "Citizenship Day" and the day for observation changed to September 17, the day the American Constitution was signed. When I lived on Long Island NY, I recall meeting someone who claimed "I am an American" day was created in Huntington Station, Long Island NY, by an immigrant grateful to be admitted to America.

The exact history of "I am an American" day does not matter, and the connection to the Melting Pot is thin, but it is noteworthy that immigrants back then expressed thanks for being admitted to America and then being able to become citizens. Publically honoring America's history isn't seen much today outside the military. I suspect today's youth never heard of the Melting Pot or assimilation in school or are even aware of these terms. Multiculturalism and diversity have become the modern mantra, with political separatists condemning the Melting Pot and assimilation.

The separation pushed by the activists, clandestinely aided by the Russians and perhaps other nations, can lead to the fall of America. Keep in mind what Abraham Lincoln said in 1858 upon his being nominated to run for the American Senate:

"A house divided against itself cannot stand."

At that time, the issue was slavery. Today it is whether Americans view themselves as being together, unified, and equal. Or whether America is split into two separate camps, the minority groups on the one hand and the mainstream group on the other hand, each going their own way. Can such a nation stand? Hopefully! But the better approach for a host of reasons presented in this book, is not to merely hope but to seek the unity, security and overall wellbeing the Melting Pot can bring.

E Pluribus Unum

E Pluribus Unum, the motto of America, appears on the Great Seal of the United States used by the Secretary of State to authenticate treaties and other documents beginning in 1782. The motto first appeared on American coinage in 1795. E Pluribus Unum also appears on the seals of the American President, Senate, House of Representatives, Supreme Court and some lesser government organizations.

The Latin "E Pluribus Unum" means "Out of many, one" although it also lends to "One from many" or "One, out of many." Translated in many ways, the gist is that the many peoples here in America will become one people, which hints at Melting Pot assimilation. However, there are other possible interpretations. For instance, the "Federalist" interpretation would be "out of many states, one country."

Yet, it now appears that officialdom on all levels of government [Federal, state and city] were doing what it could to help the immigrants to assimilate, and the immigrants wanted to assimilate. Perhaps assimilation was easier back then since immigrates mainly came from Europe with cultural backgrounds similar to those who came to America before them. They were all pushing for E Pluribus Unum, starting in 1782.

In God We Trust

The importance and continued honoring of the E Pluribus Unum motto was not conceded by everyone. In a letter sent to President Obama, written and made public by a group of legislators in Congress calling themselves the Congressional Prayer Caucus (CPC), the CPC objected to the E Pluribus

Unum motto. They maintained that the real motto of America is "In God We Trust." CPC even stated that "E Pluribus Unum is not our national motto." The "In God We Trust" motto became law in 1956, frequently said to be in support of Senator Joseph McCarthy's 1950/54 crusade against prominent Americans who were supposedly "godless" and "communists."

These activist Christian legislators were obviously of a religious group advancing their religious tenants through legislation that could be viewed as challenging America's freedom of religion history. Freedom of religion protects people who do not believe in God as well as protecting people of other religions that have religious beliefs that are not based on the Judeo-Christian God. An atheist would advocate freedom <u>from</u> religion; rather than freedom <u>of</u> religion which could imply that a person is free to choose any religion but should or must choose a religion.

The 1791 Amendment I (which was included in what is called the "Bill of Rights") to the United States Constitution states that:

> "Congress shall make no law respecting an establishment of religion or prohibiting the free exercise thereof ...."

Rights like the freedom of religion granted to the people of a country would limit the broad powers of a sovereign, whether it be the English King or the American government. Limiting the powers of a sovereign originated with the English Magna Carta of 1215, so it wasn't anything new

Rhode Island's "Royal Charter" of 1663 was the first state charter that guaranteed freedom of religion. The king at that time, King Charles II of England, allowed the Rhode Islander's to govern themselves and write a charter for their colony. However, the Virginia Declaration of Rights (adopted by the State of Virginia a few days before the signing of the Declaration of Independence on July 4, 1776) was said to the most influential in creating freedom of religion for America when the First Amendment to the Constitution became law in 1791. The Constitution was voted into law on June 21, 1788.

Passage of the First Amendment was a lengthy process because there was controversy over both having any Bill of Rights and also over granting freedom of religion. At first, the controversy was between those founders who wanted the rights to be granted by the Constitution and those founders who felt it should be left to states (or so they maintained).

Later, circa 1791, opposition to the Constitution granting the freedom of religion right arose amongst some founders because, by that time, some states already granted religious freedom in their state charters. The amended Constitution would override the state charters, which they thought to be inappropriate (or so they maintained). That argument by the "state-rights" advocates obviously failed and the freedom of religion right was included in Amendment I to the Constitution; moreover it was the first right granted in Amendment I.

Making "In God We Trust" an American motto in 1956 can be viewed as (1) imposing God on those who deny God or do not recognize that particular deity and (2) declaring that we all have trust in such God. Perhaps there was, in actual fact, no unanimity in the State of Virginia behind its Declaration of Rights which could be said to have spearheaded America's right to freedom of religion. After all, back then America was a Christian nation and there must have been some who wanted to keep it that way.

Seeing the "In God We Trust" motto every day as the American currency is used in trade could be repugnant to citizens who have other spiritual beliefs or no spiritual belief. What might be done to placate those who are offended by this motto?

They could and should be thankful that the founders of America guaranteed religious freedom to everyone in America and to those who would immigrate to America in the future. Bear in mind that America, at that time, was overwhelmingly a Christian nation. America could have then said "only Christians admitted," but it didn't. It was the age of Enlightenment, and the founders believed in religious freedom.

The founders obviously wanted people of any faith or no faith to come and be comfortable in America. The founders probably didn't contemplate that a future generation of Christians would break the founders' pledge and attempt to impose their Christian views on others.

So to those are offended by the new motto, I say you should take comfort in being correct in what you feel and say, but consider it as an incidental and minor matter to be ignored. You should also ignore the official establishment of Christmas as a national holiday. You should be thankful that your ancestors or you yourself were admitted to this Christian nation, which was then and still is a most desirable place to live. Your ancestors or you could have just as easily have been barred entrance. Accept it, be grateful, and let it be. And continue to believe as you will.

The 1956 event, when a few Christians (CPC) disgraced the founding fathers of America by pushing their God on other citizens, can be viewed as a step backwards in time. The founders cut new ground with all men being born equal, having inalienable rights, and consenting to be governed. In denying the inalienable right to freedom of religion, these God fearing Christians (righteous people as they undoubtedly were) strove to make that right alienable, and effectively started to dismantle the Constitution.

So as you accept what they did and let it be, you should nevertheless do your upmost to preserve America and what the founding fathers stood for. America still attracts the multitudes and assimilates more and more, still strives make one nation from the many, and still deserves protection against those who would deny others their rights.

Pledge of Allegiance

Campus Reform, an online publication dedicated to reporting on the conduct and misconduct of university administrators, faculty, and students, reported on January 29, 2019, that:

> "Robert Miller, president of the Santa Barbara City College Board of Trustees, said that the board would no longer be reciting the Pledge [of Allegiance],

claiming that it was 'steeped in expressions of nativism and white nationalism.' "

I rushed to check the exact wording of the Pledge of Allegiance when first officially recognized by Congress on June 22, 1942:

> "I pledge allegiance to the flag of the United States of America, and to the Republic for which it stands, one Nation indivisible, with liberty and justice for all."

I saw nothing of the "nativism and white nationalism" mentioned by Robert Miller, the college trustee, as his reason to not recite the Pledge. Nativism fosters the interests of established inhabitants against those of immigrants. In the mid 1800's, Nativists formed political parties aimed at limiting immigration and also limiting the rights of immigrants.

In addition, pledging allegiance to the flag naturally reflects patriotism, loyalty and devotion to the country all wrapped up in the term "nationalism". But why mention "white' nationalism? Color was not mentioned in the Pledge, and why create this as a distinction between Whites and presumably Blacks or other people of color? I must be missing something, so I decided to dig into the history of the pledge.

The pledge, in virtually the same words as was later adopted by Congress in 1942, was written in 1891 by Francis Bellamy, a Baptist pastor in Boston. Smithsonian Magazine's article entitled *"The Man Who Wrote Pledge of*

Allegiance" by Jeffrey Owen Jones in November 2003 pointed out that Bellamy was employed in a magazine's promotions department to arrange a patriotic school program to commemorate Christopher Columbus but there was also to be a new salute to the flag for schoolchildren as part of the project. As the salute to the flag wasn't getting done, Bellamy's boss asked him to do it and he did it.

History clearly shows that Francis Bellamy was bigoted against many of the immigrants coming to America, and could rightly be called a Nativist. He was called a Nativist by Christopher Petrella who wrote the article entitled "*The ugly history of the Pledge of Allegiance - and why it matters*" published by The Washington Post on November 3, 2017.

Mr. Petrella actually used the same combination of the terms "nativism and white nationalism" that Robert Miller later offered as the reason for his opposition to reciting the Pledge of Allegiance. It does appear that Petrella's article could have been Miller's source because the words used are unusual in themselves and the order and combination still more unusual.

It also appears that Petrella's article was an advocacy piece as it ends with the sentence:

> "The roots of the pledge shed light on the **continued necessity of protests today** that powerfully link the history of race and violence with nonnegotiable citizenship and full belonging." [Emphasis added].

It is to be noted that "Christopher Petrella teaches in the critical race, gender, and culture studies collaborative at

American University. He serves as the director of advocacy & strategic partnerships for the Antiracist Research & Policy Center, also at American University."

And yet, Mr. Petrella conceded in his article that the language in the pledge is **not overtly** nativist or xenophobic. **Not overtly** is a term meaning not visibly, not openly, or not really there. In short, there is nothing in the words of the pledge itself that is offensive, it's just the personal history of its original author that is distasteful.

What I don't understand is Mr. Petrella's purpose in raising all that muck about Pastor Bellamy. So Pastor Bellamy was a racist. Are we supposed to hate him and everything he had ever done? Otherwise why bring it up? Are we supposed to have less regard for the pledge or for America because Pastor Bellamy was a racist? Is separatism being advocated here?

Like a detective would normally inquire when investigating something that happened in his neighborhood, "**who benefits?**" from raising all that muck? Does it make for a better nation or does it aim to tear it down through separation? For all the racists there have been in America, isn't America still known around the world for being the citadel of freedom and equal treatment under law? Shouldn't we love our country ever the more for rising above the racists and others who would tear it down?

I had questioned Mr. Petrella's motives in my mind, more so when he justified adding "under God" to the pledge to show that America is against "godless communism." This is in the face of America's founders. Again "**who benefits?**" from inserting "under God" in the Pledge of Allegiance? It benefits those who are imposing their God on others and, by so doing, disgraces the founders who gave America religious freedom. It diminishes America by disgracing the founders.

It should be noted that official government instructions on how the pledge should be recited were struck down by the Supreme Court. The Supreme Court barred any compulsion to recite the pledge, barred any compulsion to attend the recital, and barred any compulsion to assume or not assume any bodily position while the pledge is recited.

As readers will later see in this book, multiculturalists have accused mainstream America of forcing minority groups to march in lock-step regimentation to do what the mainstream majority mandates, and here is an instance that disproves that accusation. The mainstream Supreme Court gets rid of regimentation when it creeps in.

Recently, the football player who kneeled during the Pledge of Allegiance before a football game instead of standing up had every right to do so, claiming he did it to protest police brutality and not to protest the Pledge. In subsequent football games other players joined in kneeling to express their beliefs, as they had every right to do based on the Supreme Court decision.

Later chapters of this book contains more on the change in the Pledge of Allegiance to insert "under God" in the Pledge and on the determination of others to oppose the Melting Pot's goal.

THE MELTING POT

America's Racism History

The Melting Pot and assimilation deals with races and racism. It aims at eliminating the blood hatreds, rivalries, feuds and vendettas carried over to America by European immigrants from their former counties. Assimilation, covered in detail in the next chapter, can be viewed as the process the Melting Pot crucible uses to create the "American."

At the time *The Melting Pot* play was written, each country of origin was treated as having its own culture and was treated as a "race." Immigrants from a foreign country tended to stick together and join those of their homeland who previously came to America. In this fashion minority groups were created and grew in America.

Each minority group was considered a "race' and was a composite of many conclaves or communities joined together in the ethnic sense of each people having a common language, cultural traits, ancestry, and history, or some combination thereof, like the German race.

The term "race" was not used in the sense of skin color, or facial or eye shape, perhaps because there wasn't much of a variance in physical attributes in Europe in that era. Europe was almost all white-skinned of no special facial or eye shape.

Thus, the author of *The Melting Pot* considered himself as being part of the Jewish race, which was discriminated against by the Russian race with their pogroms. Also according to *The Melting Pot* the German and French races, and the Irish and English races, opposed each other in the play's "racist" meaning.

These minority groups existed alongside the majority group that that spoke English and had developed the American way of doing things. The majority group can be viewed as the mainstream group that flowed out of the Melting Pot crucible that made the "American." The mainstream was constantly augmented by minority group individuals that learned English and adopted the American way of doing things. They fit-into and joined (that is, assimilating into) the mainstream group.

Thus, "racism" in Melting Pot terms could arise between one minority group and another minority group or between a minority group and the mainstream group.

Long before the Melting Pot came into existence, American racism was expressed in terms of some people, in particular the Black race, being treated unequally under law. The American goal of eliminating racism began in 1776 just before America became a nation. It started with the Declaration of Independence.

Declaration of Independence
We have to go back to 1776 and the Declaration of Independence for the origin of America's fight against racism. The preamble to the Declaration spoke in terms of

equality of people, but was essentially about the Black race. Namely, the preamble was about the black slaves and freeing them from being owned property that could be bought and sold by their white owners.

The Declaration of Independence includes this preamble:

> "We hold these truths to be self-evident, that all men are created equal, that they are endowed by their Creator with certain unalienable Rights, that among these are Life, Liberty and the pursuit of Happiness."

The Declaration of Independence was just that, a "declaration" that does not and cannot impose any law or grant any rights. Second Continental Congress meeting in Philadelphia approved the Declaration on July 4, 1776, and it was officially signed by the constituent States about a month later. The Congress thereafter addressed the writing of the Constitution which would govern the law-writing and rights-granting framework. While the Declaration did not have the force of law, its preamble established America's moral tone on addressing racism.

Thomas Jefferson

The Declaration of Independence was largely written by Thomas Jefferson and "all men are created equal" was clearly written by him. According to the historian Joseph J. Ellis in his 2018 book *"American Dialogue, The Founders and Us"* the unalienable rights portion (the " trinity of rights," originally Life, Liberty and Property) was written by another delegate with Jefferson inserting "the pursuit of Happiness" and deleting the word "Property." Jefferson's thought behind this modification was that the word "property" would include slaves and was in conflict with his desire to treat all men equally. Thus an unalienable right to own slaves could not tolerated. Jefferson's "all men are created equal" and the "trinity of rights" have become known as the American Creed.

Mr. Ellis's insights as an historian are very broad, influential and authoritative. He earned his Ph.D. at Yale University, was awarded the Pulitzer Prize for History for this very book, won other awards, but was briefly censured for exaggerating his military experience. As he showed with respect to Jefferson, nobody is perfect.

A blow-by-blow history of "all men are created equal" covering who said what and when, and how its meaning matured over time, would be interesting but in my opinion would add nothing of significance in addressing racism today. History must of necessity be interpreted under the present day surrounding circumstances the interpreter faces. In one era, history might mean one thing while it might mean something totally difference in a later era where other circumstances are paramount or simply that old may have become irrelevant.

For instance, history would show that Thomas Jefferson did believe and continue to maintain that "all men are created equal," adding that the black slaves should be free. But at the same time, history portrayed by Mr. Ellis shows that Jefferson believed and maintained that the black race was inferior. Jefferson also believed that freed blacks should be exported out of the original thirteen States to the unsettled West or to Liberia or the Caribbean Islands. So what does history actually tell us about Thomas Jefferson's fundamental beliefs? Basically, it tells us to accept and emphasize what we want at this moment in time.

Today we consider Thomas Jefferson as the great emancipator, or at least consider him the number two emancipator next to Abraham Lincoln, although Jefferson became one of the largest slave owners in Virginia and didn't free any of his slaves at the time he wrote about all men being equal and should be free.

Jefferson promised Sally Hemings, the "Black" woman he lived with for decades, that he would free their children, and he did eventually free the four children he had with her. But he never freed Sally nor the grandchildren he had through Sally. Sally was as white-skinned as could be and was of very good appearance applying white standards. She was sired by the white father of Jefferson's late, white wife. Sally and Jefferson never married although it appeared that they maintained fidelity with one another and might as well have married.

The skin color of the Blacks at Monticello, Jefferson's home, determined where they worked; the dark-skinned ones in the fields and near-white ones in the house. Like other slave owners, Jefferson eventually went bankrupt as the slave-based society failed, with over 100 dark and light-skinned slaves he owned being sold at auction to work in the cotton fields of others. His own light-skinned grandchildren became wards of the state after he died.

Since Jefferson believed that Blacks were inferior to whites and that Black blood would degrade white blood, Jefferson could be called a racist even though he believed in freeing Blacks and lived with one. While he would not accept freed Blacks continuing to live in his white society by insisting that they be expatriated, he treated Blacks with near-white skin like whites and endorsed their living in white society. So too, Native Americans could live in white society as Jefferson considered them superior to Blacks.

Abraham Lincoln

Abraham Lincoln can rightfully be viewed as the great emancipator as he did in fact liberate the slaves. However, like Thomas Jefferson, Lincoln believed that the freed slaves should be involuntarily deported according to historian Ellis. How much of a liberator is Lincoln who says you are free but get out, get away from me? So what does history actually tell us today? It depends on how you currently look at it.

Lincoln's concern with the slavery issue was exhibited early in his career when addressing his Republican political party in Illinois after having been select as its candidate for the American Senate, when he emphasized:

"A house divided against itself cannot stand."

This quoted Jesus as stated in the gospels, and Lincoln's specific purpose was to point out that the American government could not endure being half slave and half free.

Later, Lincoln asserted that ending slavery was not the purpose of the Civil War. His purpose was to keep the nation together and, consistent with this, his Emancipation Declaration can be read as a military instrument. The declaration did declare the slaves to be free, but it also enjoined them to abstain from violence [meaning they are not fight for the Confederacy] and declared that the former slaves who were physically fit would be received into the military of the United States. So what was the real purpose of the Emancipation Declaration? So what does history actually tell us today? It depends on how you look at it.

While Lincoln favored and actually took steps to explore the deportation of the freed slaves, Lincoln died before any deportation took place. White Southerners still looked down on Blacks and wanted to continue subjugating them. This evolved into the Jim Crow era with its lynchings and the Ku Klux Klan. But the Blacks were freed and millions moved North, mostly to the big cities.

Martin Luther King, Jr., the Real Emancipator

It awaited Martin Luther King, Jr. in the 20th Century to be the final and greatest emancipator who gave full meaning to all men being created equal. Reverend King's 1963 speech on the steps of the Lincoln Memorial on his March on Washington was the defining moment in the 100 year battle to effectuate Lincoln's 1863 Emancipation Proclamation and it had good press coverage.

This was the speech known as the "I Have a Dream" speech that ends with Reverend King revealing his dreams of people getting along with one another. In the speech Reverend King also sought to cash-in on what he labeled Thomas Jefferson's "promissory note." Jefferson promised equal treatment and a trinity of rights for blacks and the promises hadn't yet been honored. The speech led to the Civil Rights Act passed by Congress in 1964 and the Voting Rights Act passed in 1965.

These Federal statutes followed a number of important events in the preceding two decades, namely the 1954 *Brown v. Board of Education* Supreme Court decision that rid America of segregated public schools and President Truman desegregating the American armed services in 1948.

The Civil Rights Act and Voting Rights Act could be viewed as the final step in fully embracing Blacks in American society by effectually ending official government-condoned racism. But racism in America did not end. Blacks still lived in what could be called ghettos, didn't have the means to pursue educational opportunities and so forth. The ideal of Melting Pot assimilation as full-blooded "Americans" hadn't yet been achieved.

The Death-Blow to American Color-Based Racism

With the election of Barack Hussein Obama II, a Black, as President of the United States in 2009, a person might conclude that discrimination against Blacks was a thing of the past. This was not so. Racial discrimination against Blacks continued. It just acquired a new shape.

The election showed that mainstream white Americans would vote for a person of color who had been assimilated into mainstream American society. That is, the crucial factor in Obama being elected was that he was an assimilated Black. Never mind that he was half white, for it was his assimilation into mainstream American ways that counted. He spoke in a mainstream manner, he dressed in a mainstream manner, he had attended mainstream schools, and his family life was what one would have expected from a mainstream male. Culturally, Obama was an American. And he was self-made, a big point in the mainstream psyche. The Melting Pot crucible had worked and out came an American.

A somewhat similar event relating to religious prejudice happened in 1960 when John F. Kennedy, a Roman Catholic, was elected President of the United States. In that era, there was widespread discrimination against Catholics, particularly by Protestant groups fearing that Kennedy would take orders from the Pope. Kennedy pledged to act only in the interest of the United States and confirmed his belief in the separation of church and state. He was elected. America did in fact vote for a Catholic for the highest position in the land, and Kennedy was an assimilated American. To my personal recollection, I never again heard anything about Catholicism being a political issue.

As an aside, I remember my neighborhood caucus where Obama defeated Hillary Clinton in the Democrat primary. I had never registered as a member, nor participated in the inner-workings, of any political party in my entire life; but had to do so then in order to help my wife who became chair of my precinct's Democrat caucus. There were very few Democrats in our precinct and my wife was saddled with the job. She asked for my help. To enter the building where the caucus was held, I had to be a registered Democrat. So I registered as a Democrat, planning to register again as an independent in the next election.

I mention this because there were droves of my white mainstream neighbors registering as Democrats so that they could vote for Obama. They were all Republicans, deserting the party so that they could vote for a person of color. I could tell that they were for Obama because those who favored each candidate had to sit at opposite ends of the hall. The Clinton end of the hall was almost deserted, under a dozen persons to the eye. I discovered that a candidate had to have, as I presently recall, a minimum of 10 votes in order to appear on the precinct count. I counted only 9, so I joined the Clinton side of the hall because I felt the rout was unfairly going too far. I relate this story because I now realize how revealing and impressive an event like this should be in America's racial history.[1]

This broad acceptance of color could have been detected in the decade before Obama's election, and such acceptance accelerated in the decade after his election. For instance, colored reporters, anchors, commentators, announcers, actors and the like started to appear on TV in ever greater numbers; numbers that must have statistically exceeded the relative number of colored TV viewers if that mattered. Moreover, assimilated people of color moving into white neighborhoods no longer caused riots, but a poor, uneducated colored moving into the neighborhood might.

Along with the election of President Obama showing that people of color are now accepted by mainstream America, people of color are now being accepted and are graduating

---

[1] I guess I should mention that Hillary and Bill Clinton were schoolmates of mine since I too have a J.D. from the Yale Law School [I was 15 years earlier than them] and meet President William J. Clinton at 5-year school reunions.

America's very best universities on their own merits, without needing affirmative action programs. And people of color have risen to the very top of their professions, a broad range of professions. People of color who populate the TV broadband are perhaps the most visible to mainstream America, and they too indicate that there is little or no discrimination in America against people of color currently.

And it should be noted, if not emphasized, that all these people of color are assimilated and have been so for some time. It confirms that the Melting Pot and assimilation does work, but only to a limited extent in inner-city Black ghettos (addressed in a separate chapter).

THE MELTING POT

Assimilation

[

The term Melting Pot is a metaphor for change. The indicated change is brought about through the process of assimilation, where one thing changes into something that is similar. In the context of the Melting Pot, we are dealing with cultural assimilation where a person of one culture (frequently called the minority culture) gradually adopts and is absorbed into another culture (frequently called the majority or mainstream culture).

Cultural assimilation can be either forced or voluntary. In the ancient world, members of a captured tribe could be forced into adopting the ways of the conquering tribe and become a member of the conqueror's culture. Or the conquering tribe might allow the conquered to continue to live the way they had lived before and accept those who voluntarily adopted the conqueror's ways to join into the conqueror's cultural group. [Which is somewhat akin to the options immigrants have in coming to America.] America is governed by the rule of law which provides for liberty, freedom and equality and does not, and cannot, use forced assimilation.

There is no assimilation declaration. Nor is there any other writing that expresses what assimilation means. It means different things to different people. But we need something to start the discussion, so here is one view.

The Melting Pot crucible cannot change a person's genes. When you enter the Melting Pot crucible, you will come out still being yourself. Cloning is not to be contemplated, nor allowed. Thus, in physical terms, we would all look the way we presently look in a Melting Pot assimilated society.

The Melting Pot is frequently said to contemplate the proposition that people will become more homogenous, closer together, or more united as they go through the Melting Pot crucible. I consider this to be a lot of malarkey.

No homogenization takes place, like with the use of an electric blender ---- you will still be recognizable and not homogenized. You will not become closer together with another person, as in becoming buddies -- you will still relate to others you know as you did before. You will not be more united with others, unless you get married or join a new club. Simply put, you will still be you.

Assimilation by virtue of the Melting Pot doesn't mean you are going to be absorbed into something or integrated into something as if you were to lose your identity. Some people would say assimilation is akin to mixing a salad. Not so, each salad morsel might move to a different place in the salad bowl when the salad is mixed, but each morsel remains the same morsel.

The Melting Pot essentially changes nothing other than how a person identifies himself or herself. It's like going from saying "I am an Italian" to saying "I am an American" or, more likely, going to say "I am an American of Italian descent." It's a question of which affiliation become first in the immigrants mind. Saying I am an "Italian-American" is ambiguous, as you cannot tell which comes first in the person's mind.

There are no "politics" of assimilation. Assimilation doesn't tell the new Americans to adopt any political position, nor for that matter tell them to do anything. Besides, there is no political cohesion in America as Americans are all over of the political lot. There are two major political parties, neither of which can control their members who can stand for everything or anything. There is no requirement forcing new Americans, or any American for that matter, to join any political party or group, or adopt a particular view, or to force anyone to ignore what their inner-self evokes.

Nor is there any hierarchy or organization that controls, manages, or promotes assimilation. There are no assimilation bosses. Nobody tells an immigrant to fit-in and join the mainstream American society or how to do it. Immigrants come to fit-in on their own by doing, absorbing, and living as they did over the years, perhaps without be conscious of what was really happening; only to suddenly realize that they have come to fit-in better with the mainstream American society than with their minority society.

The process of assimilation basically connotes a cerebral recognition that a person fits into the mainstream American society. Fitting-in, like beauty, is in the eye of the beholder. All sorts of factors might be relevant, like language, speech, education, mannerisms, dress etc. And it is likely for the assimilating person to continue favoring some ethnic carryovers, like cherishing chicken parmigiana or helping their brothers or honoring their ancestors, etc.

Assimilation is essentially a subjective determination voluntarily made by the individual himself or herself. There is no assimilation stamp, certificate, visa or passport. Nor is there any official registration for the assimilated. Assimilation is an important change of self-identity, but not a divorce from one's former self.

There is no suggested pace or timeline for assimilation or, for that matter, no suggestions about anything. The most that can be said about something looking like an official suggestion would be the official adoption of the E Pluribus Unum motto ("out of the many, one") in America. The official adoption of this motto by the government could be viewed as pointing toward coming-together. It is only a motto, not a law, but is does suggest that mainstream society would embrace the assimilation of immigrants.

In assimilating, there is no requirement that the assimilated immigrant dump all the old ways and beliefs of her or his old minority group. There is no anesthetizing the individual to obliterate the past and clear the mind. The old minority group will have a friend, but not necessarily a partner, in the mainstream society for generations to come.

The tools of life change over time (like from the wheel to the auto/aircraft/spaceship, or from the radio to the TV/internet/ cellphone, etc) and so do cultures change around the world, including mainstream cultures and minority cultures. Normally the new tools bring cultures closer together and could lead to assimilations.

Individuals also change in time, and there is no requirement or inducement for assimilated individuals to always remain the same as they were when they joined the mainstream. While there is no mainstream hierarchical or control body that governs the mainstream society as a whole, or governs the various mainstream communities, hamlets, conclaves or other areas, leaders personally change over time and so too their views might change as surrounding circumstances change.

As was indicated in many ways, it is the individual who assimilates. A minority group, as such, cannot assimilate. Minority groups can merge or combine with one another, but not decide as a group to assimilate into another group. A group decision to assimilate can't work because not every individual in the group would be in a position to fit-into the other group at the same time. It would be a random joining, because individuals move at different paces.

There is no requirement for an assimilated immigrant to move out of the minority community and move into a mainstream neighborhood. Moving to a mainstream neighborhood would signal to the world that the individual had assimilated, as would merely changing dress, mannerisms and so forth. Hiding such change signals would seem to be difficult.

Assimilation does not demand intermarriage. People do tend to marry within their tribe, probably for cultural or religious reasons but also because of proximity as members of a minority group tend to live in tight-knit communities. Preferring a tribal mate is not generally considered to be racist, but that depends on how a person defines racial prejudice or discrimination.

Lack of Minority Group Cohesion

There is likely to be little cohesion in a minority group attacking assimilation, although this wouldn't be seen in the group's press releases. Inherent "conflicts of interest" could and probably do account for adverse positions on assimilation within a minority group.

A "conflict of interest" exists between parties that have opposite interests. It is "inherent" in certain types of situations. In a trade situation, the buyer inherently wants to pay a lower price and the seller inherently wants to receive a higher price. In a service-for-a-fee situation, it's inherently the same lower/higher conflict of interest. Inherent conflicts of interest lurks behind many differences of view, many arguments, and when recognized as such, can be addressed and dealt with.

In a minority group situation, the group leader could inherently strive to perpetuate her or his job, status and income while the individual members inherently want to do the best for themselves and their children as they view it. To be sure, both love and honor their group as to which there is no conflict of interest, but when it comes to assimilation of members of the group into another group, the inherent conflict of interest arises. Each is interested in what benefits them as they personally see it. And they inherently see it with different glasses.

The minority group leader inherently views assimilation as diminishing the size, status and worth of his or her group, and thus diminishing the leader personally. If assimilation continues, the leader could lose the leadership job, status and income. Some group members love and honor the group above all else, and would accord with the group leader's opposition to assimilation for a reason that differs from the leader's primary interest; for instance, the groups way of life come first with them. For others in the group, family comes first and parents might believe that their children would benefit from assimilation into the mainstream. And so forth, people differ and so do their views.

The point to be taken away from this is that the path being pursued by the leader does not necessarily have the support of most members of the group. A leader might be forcing, in one way or another, the group to comply with a path the group opposes. Whether the opposition is silent or open is up to the parties. The stakes are high.

The Arguments against Assimilation

Assimilation has been accused of being a monolith that forces members to march in lock-step. Basically, that can't be so because assimilation is the voluntary process of individuals joining a group and they would flee any inkling of lock-step regimentation. Besides, the accusation is deceptively false and misleading.

The accusation of forced regimentation, whether directed at assimilating immigrants or at minority group treatment, would be contradicted by America's Constitution and America's adherence to the rule of law. The accuser knows it. The very existence of multiculturism itself depends on receiving that equal treatment under law, which the minority groups obtain and which supports the right of their leaders to cast such spurious accusations.

Newly assimilated immigrants in the mainstream group have been accused by their former minority leaders of being mere cogs in a great wheel, demeaning the worth and position of newly assimilated immigrants and implying that they as newcomers have no real power or status in the mainstream society.

Yes, the majority group has been around for a long time, more than three centuries. Most of the people currently in the mainstream group were born into it, they didn't get up and join it the last few years. So what do the minority leaders expect? That the newcomers should control the mainstream group? Obviously, this is ridiculous as applied to any group, even the boy scouts. The newly assimilated have as much power and status as any other member of the mainstream group. They just have to take the time and work at becoming influential, a leader, or a "non-cog" just as every other assimilated person had to do.

The minority leaders' criticisms are aimed at dissuading assimilation of their members into the mainstream group, which threatens the minority leader's very existence as a leader. Dissuading assimilation suggests that political power could be at the core of the minority leader's criticism. When the newly assimilated are cast by the multiculturalists as being powerless, as being able to do nothing, and as they become a "nothing" when they assimilate, the criticism suggests that the leaders who control the multicultural dialogue are focusing on power.

The multiculturalists like to call the mainstream society the "dominant society" as they berate the mainstream majority for "dominating" minority societies in our multicultural nation. Whether the mainstream society actually "dominates" the smaller minority societies has become ever more questionable with the escalating election of many vocal and aggressive minority leaders to the American Congress. In the meantime, to be politically correct the phrase "dominate society" will be dropped in favor of using "mainstream," "mainstream society," or "majority society."

It is interesting to note that the newly elected minority leaders in Congress are today beginning to influence if not control the dialogue of the major political party they joined, to the displeasure of their mainstream compatriots in that party. The newcomers have done much in a very short period of time, perhaps indicating that the old leadership was unsuccessful in their "separation" approach as compared to the "join and fight" approach [which seems to be more of the American way].

The new crop of minority leaders appear to be diverse. Some are clearly unassimilated, publically wrapping themselves in their old flag at every opportunity. Others appear to be as assimilated as any person you just happen to meet. A few are as assimilated as could be, people you would not object to buying a house next to yours or you could actually favor that.

This could be a good trend, but hopefully not go too far. Going too far can lead to extreme resentment, hatred and increased political partisanship; ending with a divided nation; a nation that cannot stand for long, especially today with foreign nations (e.g. Russia) secretly interfering in ways aimed at increasing divisions within America and destroying America.

Mainstream society is an open society of people, notwithstanding their different backgrounds, who fit-in with one another. They would hope and expect to remain that way as the individual members grow, change, and modify views.

Some proponents of multiculturalism try to make the mainstream society into some sort of confederation that determines everything for everybody. And then, that mainstream "confederation" is accused of controlling the body politic, making laws that favor themselves and disadvantage the minority groups and their members.

America is still a land where the rule of law controls, and the basic morality of equal treatment under law prevails. All citizens can vote, whether they are assimilated into the mainstream or remain in a minority group. Both the assimilated and unassimilated are free to have their own views on issues and free to openly express them.

The mainstream is made up of assimilated individuals from many minority groups and those individuals could and probably do have a variety of views because of their differing cultural backgrounds. To assimilate an individual does not have to deny everything her or his ethnic culture believed. The assimilated can support the views of the minority groups they left.

Although the mainstream is being accused of being intractably undividable and controlling the body politic, the real world shows that there is little cohesion in the mainstream. As previously stated, there is a great diversity of opinion based on the assimilated retaining some of their former minority cultural views. Aside from that, there are many shades of political views in the majority group; from liberal to conservative plus some in-between or at the extremes. The assimilated have and continue to join a variety of political parties or political groups and have done so for some time as their ancestors immigrated to America and assimilated.

Recent events, that even includes extraordinary government shut-downs, proves that there is little consensus within the mainstream group. So the ranting by a minority group leader against a dominate monolith, that obviously doesn't exist, serves to really target and propagandize members of the leaders own group as the leader strives to keep the group together and retain leadership.

Also, there can be no doubt that the actual legislation we have seen in recent decades included many programs aimed at helping the needy, improve job readiness, educate, bolster health of all members of society including those in minority groups on an equal basis. If any discrimination is to be found in mainstream society it would be found in mainstream university and college affirmative action programs aimed at helping minority groups that needed help and in government programs to help Native Americans. Both programs have been successful, the affirmative action programs successful enough to recently cause those discriminated against to go to court to stop the discrimination.

The mainstream group would normally expect to be the main voice in the body politic if it is larger than the minority groups taken together. This still appears to be the case today. But it wouldn't be so in the future if positions reverse and the minority groups become the larger. Either way, it can never be one group terrorizing the other legally as long as equal treatment remains Constitutional law.

Leadership, Power and Politics

This mainstream emphasis on helping individuals does not please some minority group leaders who would rather see the mainstream help flow to their groups for redistribution instead of flowing directly to the individuals in their groups.

These leaders argue and try to induce mainstream society to funnel all individual help, and they also specify any "rewards" and "benefits" of any kind, to their groups so that the leaders, who supposedly know their members better and love them more, could decide on fair distribution.

At the same time, power hungry minority leaders adopted new approaches to hinder their loss of adherents through assimilation. This was the adoption of their "politics of difference," sometimes also called the "politics of diversity" or the "politics of identity."

Whatever the new politics is called, the purpose was to make their minority members more different and distant from those in the mainstream society so as to make assimilation less likely. For instance, some minority leaders induced member to adopt the ways, dress, grooming, outlook and mannerisms of the ancient society that neither they nor generations of their ancestors ever knew. These leaders sometimes went to extremes in imposing "separate by differentiation" on their minority group.

In America's history, racists had used a "separate but equal" catchphrase claim. The claim was that racial segregation into separate facilities that were "equal" did not violate the equal protection provision of the Constitution. The minority groups fought this false equality and won in an assimilated court, the Supreme Court. So much for the proposition that the "dominant" assimilated mainstream society's aim was to suppress the minority groups. The assimilated Supreme Court voted in favor to the minority group.

Neither does a "separate and apart" catchphrase apply even though the minority leaders would like nothing better for their groups to be separate and apart from the mainstream and other minority groups. That catchphrase usually refers to a marital split-up awaiting divorce although it could be a test as to whether separating and being apart is to be preferred to staying together. The minority leaders don't want to test anything, they know they want their group to be separate.

That's what their "separate by differentiation" slogan stands for. It has nothing to do with equality because it actually goes in the opposite direction. Separate is never equal. The slogan is wrapped entirely in power and politics, as the minority leaders implicitly acknowledge when they call it the "politics of difference."

Their political action is to drive their minority group and its members to create and embrace unsurmountable cultural differences (at the risk of destroying personal identities of some of their people) so as to assure permanent separation from the mainstream society and, of course, perpetuate their leadership and derive ever more power from their groups' legislative votes.

Helping Blacks Escape Inner-City Ghettos

In my view, one of the most important problems facing America is its ghettoes. It is the problem that telescopes what's wrong with America in the most fundamental ways that must be rectified if America is to move forward. Not all the ghettos are inner-city, nor are they all African-American or colored, with there being some indication that White ghettos may be the largest group.

I simply use the African-American inner-city ghetto as a proxy for all the American ghettos, because it has the full roster of problems and has been the most intractable. It shouldn't be that in as much as African-Americans, in terms of aggregate numbers, have been in America longer than any other group except Native Americans. The common denominator in all the ghettos is poverty.

The African-American ghettos were caused by extreme poverty and perpetuated by racial discrimination. This contrasts with immigrants coming to a new and strange land seeking to live with their own people in the cheapest space available before their intended assimilation; when overcrowded that space turned into ghettos. Others faced restrictions or opposition to their living elsewhere in America and forced them to live in the most undesirable area, the local ghetto.

Whoever the inhabitants of ghettos are, they all or almost all want out and face obstacles to it. Assimilation would be the way out, but obstructions have been constructed.

The ghetto had taken on a new life of its own since it first came on the scene some 500 years ago. The medieval city-state of Venice in Catholic Italy, forced Jews to live in a restricted run-down former foundry area because their ways and religion were alien to the rich and religious Venetians. The Venetian word for foundry led to the word ghetto in English. It was a virtual jail area for Jews. Other European city-states and countries soon adopted similar segregation laws. Today's ghettos are not jails, do not represent legally forced segregation and are generally not religiously based.

Today, America's mainstream society genuinely tries to help the ghettos. There are welfare programs, educational programs, job assistance programs, family assistance programs and a host of other programs specially designed to improve conditions in the ghettos and help ghetto residents leave the ghettos. And it has become apparent that those programs aren't doing the job.

West Side Story, the Musical

A musical about a mixed ghetto, West Side Story, opened on Broadway in New York City in 1957 and won choreography and design awards but not best musical. It was followed in 1961 by a film adoption that won 10 academy awards including best picture. The movie is an easily available (video, Netflix) brilliant Romeo & Juliet mixed-race teenage love story getting caught up with ethnic gangs competing to control ghetto turf, with conflict being fueled by chance mishaps and misinformation. Basically it's a story of juvenile delinquency leading to a tragic ending, beautifully surrounded by brilliant music, lyrics and dance. At the end, there is the vague suggestion that tragedy unites as the two gangs leave a murder scene.

The movie is also a masterful political film dealing basically with Melting Pot and assimilation issues that would likely have made a huge impression on a public which would not ordinarily seek political entertainment. The sheer brilliance, confirmed by the awards, public attendance and public approval shows that it must have had an outsized impact on the American psych.

One gang was of first generation Polish-Americans and the other were Puerto Ricans who recently moved to that Manhattan ghetto. Puerto Ricans were made American citizens back in 1917 so they have a right to move to America without going through the normal immigration process.

The two groups didn't like each other and competed, but seemed to have agreed

to some rules of conduct. But events conspired to create actual conflict and killings.

That is exactly what the Melting Pot and assimilation aimed to stop. The musical did its share in terms of its plot. It also cut new ground by using actors of different nationalities on the American stage, exhibiting mixed-race love before anti-miscegenation laws were declared unconstitutional by the Supreme Court in 1967, and other things that were new at the time. And it was a heterosexual love musical written by assimilated gays, who in that era may have been subject to the most discrimination. But what the musical did most of all, was to alerted society that race conflict is potentially dangerous and society should do more to combat it.

The musical also did that by ridiculing police offer Sargent Krupke, who was cast to show that officialdom was then ineffective and uncaring when it came to ghettos. And this too was done in a brilliant way.

The Polish-American gang was taunting Sargent Krupke musically, making statements that truly and insightfully represented the problems faced by ghetto residents; like stating it was their upbringing that caused them to act badly, pointing out that their mothers were junkies and their fathers were drunks, so naturally they would be punks. Another musical taunt stated they never got the love children needed so that they were misunderstood, that they were not delinquents and good is to be found deep down in them. All this was serious social commentary presented in a light spirit, beautifully staged, musically superb and very telling.

This must have made a huge impression on a segment of the American public not remotely aware of what was truly going on in the ghettos or what was at stake, except for reading about gang murders in the newspapers.

The Recent Record in Exiting Ghettos
On all counts except one, mainstream society has been relatively successful in helping minority groups elevate themselves through a variety of programs having that very

46

purpose. The exception has been in dealing with the inner-city ghettos where the otherwise successful programs have failed. This suggests that America prioritize addressing the inner-city problems, continue the old assistance programs as they now are without even trying to improve them while efforts and treasure are devoted to developing new approaches.

As previous said, Martin Luther King did what was politically needed in his time, namely change the way government treated Blacks and other people of color and open opportunities for them. However, Reverend King's political leveling of the playing field did not immediately do much if anything to economically benefit Blacks, particularly in the South where most Blacks lived and faced continued race discrimination.

Millions of Blacks started exiting to the cities of the North; also finding discrimination there because of their skin color, because of their cultural differences, and because they couldn't have learned much during the decades of slavery. This changed over time as Blacks got educated, got better jobs, and left their ghettos. While anti-Black discrimination continued to exist over the decades, America and its states and cities did enact special assistance and affirmative action programs to aid the deprived, which improved the status and well-being of millions of Blacks over time.

But the inner-city Black ghetto's somehow managed to survive, grow and become a major problem of the African-American community, recently compounded by the loss of political power to the fast growing Hispanic/Latino/Chicano-American communities.

The residents of today's inner-city ghettos are the Blacks with little resources and no family members in a position to help them. They are the Blacks who didn't or couldn't benefit from years of special and affirmative action programs. Poverty forced them into the most abject ghettos and racial discrimination kept them there.

Mainstream Whites might look down on the actions, abject poverty and squalor of those Blacks and actually pity them, but they generally did not seek to abuse the downtrodden. There were some Whites who openly abused Blacks, like when White workers encounter Black workers in the workplace and abused them for taking jobs away from Whites. Recently, it seems that such abuse is directed against Hispanic immigrants accused of taking White jobs. Nevertheless, it does appear that such discrimination is based on job competition, and not based on color discrimination which almost disappeared when President Obama was elected.

The first question I asked myself was what distinguished the present-day ghetto residents from former ghetto residents who appeared to have benefited more from the affirmation action and other programs that lifted them out of the ghettos. They were all very poor. The ghetto street life and camaraderie wouldn't have been very different then and now. Perhaps today's youth wouldn't attend or take those programs seriously. Perhaps the programs weren't tailored to today's ghetto youths. Perhaps the programs aren't properly staffed now.

Yet, the present generation of ghetto residents probably had access to more and better help programs, better schools, better transportation, and better communications, including the newest gadget, cellphones. In short, it appeared to me that the current ghetto residents have it "better" than the former ghetto residents who escaped the ghettos say a decade ago.

That underlies my reason for suggesting that the old programs be left as they are while all efforts are devoted to developing new approaches to help the ghettos. Perhaps the first order of business would be having professionals compare previous and present conditions to confirm that relatively more inhabitants were escaping the ghettos previously than now and whether conditions and programs were comparable.

Searching for Solutions

1). Parental guidance could be the key to raising children as I think was the case with my growing up in a virtual ghetto. I refer back to the time my parents, then unmarried, came to America, uneducated and poor. When I was born, they were still poor, but they did take classes to learn English. We were poor, not in abject poverty, yet I never realized I was deprived as a child according to modern standards. Everything seemed okay to me and such thoughts never arose, probably because I had family support and guidance.

Perhaps family life and parent-child relationships in the ghettos deteriorated in the last generation and that accounted for the recent lack of progress. For example, could it be that the increasing use of drugs in the ghettos, particularly by mothers, resulted in a deterioration of family life and child-raising. Perhaps this kept the children from developing social skills and all the things that would help the children escape the ghetto. Whatever is actually at work in the ghetto in this area should be uncovered.

Addressing family/parental relations in the inner-cities could prove to be as important as addressing poverty. Social scientists and psychologist's deal with this and I'd suggest they develop totally new approaches instead of reworking old ones that were lacking.

2). I suppose there was some sort of informal code of conduct in my slum community but if there was anything like it, it was nothing that personally impacted me. We'd play stickball on certain streets, pick teams in a certain way, and otherwise hang out together, but nobody told us how to dress, talk or carry ourselves and there was no pecking order to respect. It was nothing like the "code of the street" as described by the University of Pennsylvania professor of social science Elijah Anderson in his book *"Code of the Street, Decency, Violence, and the Moral Life of the Inner City"* published in 1999, two decades ago.

What particularly surprised me was Professor Anderson pointing out that there were essentially two cultures in the Germantown Avenue (Philadelphia) ghetto he studied; one consisting of the "street" families and one of "decent" families. The decent families aimed to assimilate into mainstream society and the street families basically aimed to please the ghetto gang leaders. If this is generally the case in today's ghettos, it requires separate and distinct plans designed to help each of the duo-ghettos.

The code of the street seems to be extensive, covering even minor things like eye contact. Studying how the street code developed might help in devising ways to dismantle the code or ways to deal with it. All such studies should be conducted by independent, credentialed professions, not by the un-credentialed who are said to know the ghetto better.

3). The role of a "leader" interested me from my slum days. The most liked and respected person was the local bookie. I got this by the way my father reacted to the man. My father didn't place bets or talk with him, but even a kid could tell that the bookie was the boss. I had no idea what made him the boss or whether he was good or bad. I didn't then think in those terms.

Now I look at things with different glasses. When I consider all the cheating, including law breaking, by some large reputable corporations, by some of rich elite, and by some of our legislators, I can't help but wonder what's going on in the ghettos. To be sure, the ghettos are poor. Yet loads of economic activity takes place in ghettos, and loads of money must go through the ghettos. As with any activity there must be the good and the bad.

Ghettos are just conclaves or communities in an officially recognized city, county or administrative area . So ghetto leadership might be dual. There is; the unofficial ghetto community leadership (the gang leaders) and the official political leadership. They can be one and the same. I have no idea how the ghetto gang leadership is structured, what is actually going on in the ghettos, whether it is at all interesting, or whether it can even be uncovered. It probably falls within the bailiwick of investigative reporting or someone like Professor Anderson, but someone should be studying it.

The following was taken from an FBI website:

> "2 years ago   An estimated one million gang members are perpetrating violence in America's schools and neighborhoods. They could be infiltrating your very own community. The FBI calls them 'urban terrorists.' "

I am not sure I got to the right FBI online page or whether it relates to what I seek. But it'll do in terms of showing that gangs are numerous and that gangs seems to be a separate investigative area for law enforcement. The gangs I expect within a ghetto are those made up of ghetto residents and deal only with residents of that particular ghetto. I am not referring to an Al Capone type gang. And perhaps there is more than one gang in a ghetto, a la the West Side Story. Nor am interested in what the gangs do other than what, if anything, they do that directly or indirectly impacts Melting Pot and assimilation considerations of ghetto members.

With all the gangs that exist and seem to be growing, ghetto gang leadership, and their relationships within and without the ghettos should be explored. It would again be a question of "**who benefits?**" from the existing ghetto situation and the way things work in the ghetto. Meaningful changes in a predatory gang leadership, if that proves to be the case, would probably do wonders. Where the gang leaders do a benevolent job, they should be blessed and the social scientists or investigative reporters go on to examine other aspects of ghetto life.

4). Something just happened that could materially help the inner-city ghettos. Many inner-city youths wind-up facing long jail sentences for non-violent crimes, frequently drug related. These excessively long sentences were legislated decades ago by those who thought the long sentences would deter drug crimes. It didn't work. Increasing the number and length of inner-city incarcerations made rehabilitation more difficult and wrecked many if not most career paths for those incarcerated. The former inmates wound up having no option other than doing more of the same.

What happened just last month was that our very partisan Congress went bipartisan (a rare event) to lower the sentencing terms which should reduce incarcerations of ghetto residents. It wasn't a trade-off deal where each political party gives the other something they want, but it was true bipartisanship where they actually worked together in determining the right thing to do.

Incidentally, this once again shows that mainstream society can and does work in unison to help the depressed [and this again counters arguments that the mainstream aims to dominate and destroy minority groups]. This suggests that we should develop ancillary programs bootstrapping off the new legislation. For instance, is there anything that can now be done to really get our jails to rehabilitate inmates?

I recall that there was once a suggestion that inmates who did well in some jail courses be sent to local colleges to continue their academic work while they served out their sentences. This created a backlash by parents complaining that they had to pay for sending their kids to college.

I don't recall what happened to this suggestion, and I mention it for a purpose. Those jail courses worked in terms of improving the academic skills of inmates, as shown by some inmates becoming ready for college. Perhaps it was only those inmates who already had such academic skills benefited, but it is likely that others benefited as well.

It would seem that more courses teaching academics, reasoning, verbal and arguing skills would go far in providing intellectual skills instead of just pushing mechanical skills in our jails. Substituting discussion and friendly argumentation for fisticuffs should improve an inmate's social skills and self-image. How many inner-city youths were exposed to discussion/argument at the dinner table at home? Based on my limited knowledge in this psychologist/social scientist bailiwick, I can merely suggest that more attention be directed to family relationships in the very early years of a child's upbringing and bolster that approach in the jails.

At this point in time, society needs to employ the people and spend the treasure needed to do the job -- the job is to change the ghettos and make the inner-cities desirable places to live. Again, at this point in time I suggest expending funds initially only on creative research and original brainstorming by ticketed professionals.

5). Growing success in what ghetto youth had been doing is a new factor impacting ghettos. It is elevating the status of ghetto and allowing ghetto youths to earn meaningful reputations in dance, music and to a lesser extent art. In dance, there is hip-hop, breakdancing and more. In music, there is rap, reggae and more that I couldn't describe. Each of the top rap singers in 2018 earned in the tens of millions of dollars, clearly something to strive for and ghetto youth have or can have the credentials.

Ghetto youth have been preforming in both in and outside of the ghettos, doing well but I suspect not on the million dollar level. Ghettos might become interesting and creative place to live. There must be a new vitality in such ghettos, probably changing the ghettos. I would like to assume that this will aid the Melting Pot and assimilation, but I'm fearful of increased ghetto efforts to combat assimilation.

As discussed earlier, there are minority group leaders who work against assimilation that would shrink the minority group as members exit to mainstream society, and thus diminish their own status, self-image, and potentially their economic well-being. Many multiculturalists argue for and literally demand that minority groups do more to separate themselves from mainstream society by creating ever more separation by maximizing differences. And so too, perhaps, with ghetto gang leaders. Researchers, social scientists, psychologists etc should keep this in mind as they explore ways to help the ghetto.

Here's something out-of-the-box that might work in a ghetto strong in the performing arts. With the preforming arts off and running in the ghetto, perhaps officialdom or a philanthropist would be willing to fund the construction in a ghetto of a performing arts theater that would serve two purposes: (A) provide a first-class stage for ghetto performers and youthful ghetto aspirants, and (B) provide a beginners' training ground to create interest and start helping non-preforming ghetto youths learn construction skills, stage hand skills, theater maintenance and administration skills and the like. Having a ghetto youth at a professional's side (as a requirement for the professional accepting work on this project) as the theater is being built should spark interest and increase the youth's self-worth, and more. It would slow the construction and other activities somewhat, but what better and cheaper way is there to show ghetto youth what goes on in the outer-world and how they might participate in it?

Multiculturalism

Multiculturalism essentially refers to a number of minority groups of different cultures living separately within the majority mainstream America society. Having many cultures extols the "open" American society in contrast to an essentially "closed" society, like the ancient Japanese society. America was never closed, unless you focus on the time when only Native Americans occupied the land, and even then there were tribes with very different cultures. After that time, America became a land of immigrants as people of different cultures moved in and America became destined to forever be an "open" society.

Although general harmony exists between the various minority cultural groups living in America today, some intergroup discrimination exists. In its simplest form, it could merely be based and not liking the "other." Should old world's blood hatreds, rivalries, feuds and vendettas have traveled to America with a minority group, intergroup discrimination could be much more serious, possibly leading to actual conflict.

The term "multiculturalism" indicates, at a minimum, that the minority groups consider their cultures to be more important than the assimilated Melting Pot mainstream culture and look to forever being separate and apart from the mainstream culture. That is, they merely want to be left alone to continue to live their cultures. But at the extreme, the multiculturalists want to change the mainstream culture to their liking or, much worse extreme, eliminate the existence of the mainstream culture.

Some minority groups feel that they are being discriminated against by the mainstream, with some minority groups discriminating in return because of their treatment or some just seeking fulfillment of the promise of equal treatment under the Constitution. Some minority groups have little internal cohesion where members are free to speak their minds, and some are more regimented. Some minority groups, or specifically their leaders, seek to maximize the group's cultural differences with the mainstream society so as to assure continued separation and non-assimilation of their people.

It's a mixed bag, as there is no hierarchical or control body presenting the multicultural views or positions. Each minority group, or its leaders, stake out their own positions, possibly joining with some others, possibly not. However, they all truly favor multiculturalism as a concept although they might differs in the details.

In discussing multiculturalism, the term "multiculturalist(s)" is used here as referring to just the one voice of a minority group speaking out for the group and being treated as the presentative or leader of the group. The term "multiculturalist(s)" does not refer to all minority groups or to the concept of multiculturalism itself since there is no multicultural hierarchy or leadership that can speak for all minority groups and views could and do differ between groups or even within a group.

Separatism and "Politics of Difference" verses "Politics of Assimilation"

As will be shown, much of the multicultural rhetoric specifically revolves about power and politics which ultimately reflects the view of the political leaders of the minority groups.

In America, political power rests basically in three official power centers: Federal, state and city where there can be just so many political leaders and some of those seats are filled by those minority group leaders. There might also be other official power centers or administrative areas, also lead by local political leaders. Leaders galore!

Each minority group can be viewed as being separate political power center in itself and the number of potential political leaders expands exponentially. Particularly so when a minority group is dispersed in many locations within a number of states and cities with each having its own leaders. Where a minority group has many locations, it could have a centralized board or council. Super galore!

As can be seen in the use of the phrases "Politics of Difference" verses "Politics of Assimilation, instead of using just "Difference" verses "Assimilation" the subject matter is being treated as political.

The multiculturalists' pitting the Politics of Difference against the Politics of Assimilation clearly aims at reinforcing and expanding minority cultural identification so as to create ever more separation from mainstream society. For instance, ancient ways of dressing and adornment could be reintroduced to the minority group, and its present day culture made to adopt it and become more different and more separate from the mainstream culture. There is no combining of the different cultural heritages. Each minority group, in accordance with the way they define themselves, look back to its own cultural heritage.

However, it is possible for a minority group, like African-Americans, to create some type of melding of African cultures since some or many African-Americans don't know what African tribe they came from. In that situation, an ancient culture has been newly created and not actually reintroduced.

The only other blending of cultures I am aware of is actually the mainstream culture itself because assimilation didn't and doesn't now require the assimilated to dump cultural traits. For example, those who call themselves Italian-Americans, or Americans of Italian Descent, seem to be assimilated but still hold on to at least parts of their Italian heritage.

All this differentiation, whether actually reintroduced or just recently re-blended, is contemplated in the Politics of Difference and is the tool of separatism. The goal is separation from the mainstream and also separation from other minority groups.

I didn't research where and how this separatism drive actually originated since that isn't really meaningful. What is meaningful is that, however originated, it seems to have been widely accepted amongst minority groups.

It seems to have become a generalized multiculturalist position, but one that has or could have dissimilar treatment in different minority groups in keeping having different ancestors and different life styles. Some minority groups might actually favor and aim at assimilation as shown in previous generations of their immigrants coming to America, the new country, for the very purpose of assimilating. Others just wanted the freedom to live their culture in America, free of oppression.

Also a person might question whether any return to or recovery of ancient ways is even possible because surrounding conditions would have changed materially in the meantime, particularly in coming to America. Obviously, returning to an ancient type hut and living amongst animals not realist nor can it really be the purpose.

So the minority group is faced with choosing an era to "revert" to. Basically the separatism of recapturing the ancient ways is not that simple and could lead to adopting something newly developed as a substitute.

It is not clear that all or even most minority groups, or the people within those groups, oppose assimilation. Yet, the multiculturalist had to have an opponent, or set one up, to make their case, and Melting Pot assimilation was available to be cast into that role.

The multiculturalists concocted the phrase the phase "Politics of Assimilation" to join the issue although assimilation isn't generally considered to be a political matter.

Nor is there any assimilation hierarchy or control group that could write any manifesto that could be called the Politics of

Assimilation. There are no politics of assimilation. Assimilation is merely a process which changes in time as conditions change. Thus, it is the multiculturists who have made up and written the "Politics of Assimilation" on behalf of the assimilated, which is akin to having a wolf write the hen-house operating manual.

While the advocates of Politics of Difference might merely be seeking power, it would be interesting to see what they actually say to condemn assimilation and what might be said in response.[2]

The Politics of Difference advocates claim that (while conceding the law does apply equally to all) the rules and policies of assimilation (1) deny the importance of separate cultural groups or see them as undesirable, (2) were made by others without the participation of the separate cultural groups, (3) make the cultural groups that don't meet the requirements appear deviant or abnormal and (4) that a cultural group that is unable to comply creates feelings of inadequacy, internalizing, self-hate, and ambivalence.

(1). In response, it should again be pointed out that there are no legal, nor even any informal, compilation of any rules and policies of assimilation. Assimilation is an individual act of just fitting in with the ways of a different societal group (the mainstream group) and yet not having to abandon all the ways of, or regard for, her or his previous minority cultural

---

[2] For this I use the essay *Social Movements and the Politics of Difference* by Cheryl Zarlenga Kerchis and Iris Marion Young, which appears in the book *Multiculturalism from the Margins ; Non-Dominant Voices on Difference and Diversity* edited by Dean A. Harris, 1995.

group. These individuals are in the mainstream today along with a whole line of immigrants from many cultures that came to America with the view of assimilating, also not totally abandoning the some of the old ways, beliefs and regard for the old culture.

Thus, it is doubtful that mainstream society would think of minority groups as being unimportant or undesirable, using as support the fact that everybody in the mainstream came from minority groups at one time or another. And it is unlikely that they abandoned all their old ways and regard for their previous minority groups. I could find no support for multiculturalists maintaining the opposite.

(2). While the separate cultural groups could not have written the laws they faced when they immigrated to America, nor necessarily participated in writing the laws while they were in America, they are of course free to try to change any law they do not like. But the only relevant laws I know in the context of what is being discussed here are based on equality, equal treatment for everybody, which the multiculturist writers of Politics of Difference say they support.

(3). There are no requirements for assimilation. They don't exist. There is no pass or fail test to be taken for assimilating. If the multiculturalists know of requirements, they should be delineated.

(4) Again, there is nothing a minority cultural group has to comply with in order to assimilate. Besides, the group itself doesn't assimilate, only individual members of the group assimilate. As a minority group itself does not even attempt

to assimilate, there can be no failure or inability of the group itself to pass muster in any way, to feel deviant or feel inadequate in any way.

The concept of Melting Pot assimilation, and the motto "of many, one" extols joining together over separatism as the better way while not saying anything to deny or brand the separate cultural groups as being unworthy, to say nothing of creating feelings of inadequacy, internalizing, self-hate, and ambivalence.

That's quite a roster of negative feelings. How can the group members be so miserable? If a minority group should feel all that, the minority group itself would be failing their members.

Or could it be that each proposition actually works in the opposite direction? Perhaps, the adoption of ancestral ways of dress, of grooming and the like by the un-assimilated becomes an unwelcome burden, pre-empting other things that could be done and creating unhappiness in minority communities. And perhaps the assimilated with high-paid jobs and higher mortgages are very unhappy. I suspect that even if there is some truth in these "reversals" it would not change anything anybody in either group believes.

I tried and failed to find statistics addressing whether the separatists actually did help the minority groups advance or whether the mainstream governmental programs helped more or less than the minority groups. It would be even more difficult to statistically address whether the separatists did more for the minority communities in terms of enhancing how the people see themselves, improving their social-lives and increasing happiness than the mainstream society did through its affirmative action and other programs.

Seeking Power; Black Power

The multiculturalists advocate cultural separation and the Politics of Difference as essentially a better strategy to achieve political power than assimilation could deliver. This must have played out in many ways, most publically and forcefully in the African-American community.

It led to the Black Power movement which was opposed by Martin Luther King, Jr. because it contemplated violence and separatism. Reverend King was the foremost leader of the civil rights movement that looked to improve the status of all American citizens, White as well as Black, by non-violent means and he largely succeeded in his efforts. Reverend King was responsible for the enactment of the civil and voting rights acts of 1964/65 that virtually eliminated racial differentiation in politics and in the workplace, and made for equality.

Some reputable Black organizations agreed with the Black Power movement and dropped non-violence from their charters, while others stuck to non-violence. The NAACP publically denounced the Black Power movement. "Black is beautiful" became a slogan. The "Black Panther Party for Self-Defense" was formed, and the Black Power movement won the hearts of the Black community.

The Black Panther Party revealed its political purpose, which was much broader than merely helping the Black community. The Black Panther Party declared its belief in an extreme form of socialism or communism in its October 1966 Platform & Program:

> "We believe the federal government is responsible and obligated to give every man employment or a guaranteed income. We believe that if the white American businessmen will not give full employment, then the means of production should be taken from the businessmen and placed in the community so that the people of the community can organize and employ all of its people and give a high standard of living."[3]

The Black Power movement and Black Panther Party failed, but their separation-by-difference policy was resurrected in recent years as African-Americans, particularly those in inner-city ghettos, hadn't made sufficient economic or educational progress even though many government programs were specifically aimed at that. Yet, significant numbers of Blacks did benefit from these programs, joined the middle class, and were able to and did assimilate into mainstream society. Mainstream society was becoming less White and the Black communities were diminished somewhat.

---

[3] Shades of this could be read into today's events as the newly elected Latino-American Congresswoman Alexandria Ocasio-Cortez is being labelled a socialist or communist because she believes in large tax increases on the very wealthy to fund social assistance programs for the poor and because of her proposed Green New Deal resolution. One begins to wonder whether there is going to be a Latino Power Party and other such political parties in the future, which would be constitutionally allowed and hopefully not violent.

This exodus was said to weaken the Black communities, again inducing multiculturalists to condemn assimilation and advocate ever greater separation differences.

Lack of Cohesion

Many if not most cultural groups have their better-off and their poor, their educated and uneducated, their skilled and non-skilled, their workers and shirkers, their satisfied and unsatisfied, their law-abiding and their criminals and so forth.

And there are groups with varying views and beliefs within the various cultural groups. There are groups that have splits within, whether they are based on ethnicity, race or religion. Perhaps religion is the greatest unifier, but the lack of cohesion exists even there.

To illustrate at what could be the extreme, the Jews have their major Orthodox, Conservative, and Reform groups, and also have the smaller Reconstructionists, Karaites, and Hasidim groups, each with their own rabbis and separate ordination bodies, each with their own places of worship. The Hasidim stand out in terms of appearing different with their ancient dress code, required hair styling and discrimination against women, and in terms of embarrassing the more modern Jewish groups and becoming a reference point for anti-Semites. At the other extremes are Jews of limited faith and the Nobel Prize winners, but they are likely to have been assimilated along with individual members of the major and smaller groups except for the Hasidim.

India has multitude of religious groups, too numerous to number, which are trying to find a basis to act and appear as one cultural group, a brave move if it can be accomplished.

On average, based on overall immigration to America, the African-Americans were here in America longer than any other group except for the Native Americans. The years of enslavement did little or nothing for their personal growth and development, but after emancipation Blacks did develop and separate into their own class divisions. Those forced by poverty to live in the ghetto-like inner-cities can be viewed as having developed still another new culture in addition to their post-slavery culture.

Indicative of what could be the birth of a new culture, by the 1960's the inner-city Blacks had developed their own way of speaking called Ebonics. The mainstream Black community, led by the NAACP, deprecated Ebonics as did professional linguists. Ebonics as a new language fell by the wayside although it continued to be used in African-American communities. In 1996, the Oakland [California] School Board recognized Ebonics as the primary language of most of its African-American students and while the board wouldn't teach Ebonics, the board would respect Ebonics and take it into account in its teaching.

Thus, each multicultural minority group in America does not necessarily speak to the world with one voice nor necessarily have cohesion and agreement within the group. And the group itself is subject to change over time, or to develop subgroups that take on independent status. And, with the passage of time, individuals leave these groups as they assimilate into the American mainstream. America has no official language, which help to perpetuate multiculturalism.

Diversity Strengthens America

Diversity in America, and multiculturalism in America, are largely synonymous. Each cultural group making up America's multiculturalist society is necessarily different from one another, which is what diversity signifies. Thus the terms "diversity" and "multiculturalism" are essentially redundant.

It is not clear whether an assimilated society on the one side or a multicultural/diversified society on the other side strengthens America more. Fortunately, we don't have to address this question. It is talent that strengthens America, and talent resides in individuals. A group may include talented individuals and be considered a talented group, but the talent still resides in the talented individuals.

Thus, it makes no difference whether the talented writer, musician, dancer, scientist, mathematician, teacher or entrepreneur is of a minority cultural group or is of the assimilated majority group in terms of America being strengthened. It is the individual being in America and it is the individual's inherited genes, skills and talents that are important in terms of strengthening America, not where the individual came from or what group the individual belongs to.

That being the case, it cannot be said that diversity justifies multiculturalism, as the terms are synonymous. What strengthens America are the talents of all the individuals in

America, irrespective of minority group or mainstream association.

Advantages and Disadvantages

The advantages of multiculturalism are basically that it has made America a "richer" and more interesting society by bringing a number of foreign cultures closer or into the American landscape. "Richer" in terms of having more different styles of houses of worship, more different kinds of restaurants, more different styles of dances on the dance floor and so forth.

In a sense, it was the act of immigration itself that brought these advantages to America. These advantages would have been here in America had the concept of multiculturalism not invaded the land. The assimilated from the respective cultures really deserve the credit for introducing the cultural dance styles to the dance floor, opening the culture-based restaurants, and building a mixture of houses of worship.

It was the immigration into America of the different cultural groups that brought all this about, not the concept of multiculturalism. They came for the advantages of America as they saw them, not to create multiculturalism in America.

The disadvantages of multiculturalism are basically that the immigrating cultural groups also brought to America some of the old country hatreds, rivalries, feuds and vendettas against other immigrant cultural groups that potentially or actually creates frictions or even conflicts in America. This is exactly what the Melting Pot aimed to stop.

Also, the exponential growth of one or more minority cultural groups could be viewed as changing the fabric of America, causing resentment or hostility in other minority groups that hadn't immigrated America for this changed America, or with those in the assimilated mainstream group who feel the same way. Minority cultural groups also change in time and become somewhat more Americanized (that is, slightly assimilated) or on the other hand deliberately differentiate themselves more as encouraged by the multiculturists. As long as this does not lead to violence, as did the Black Power movement, everything is fine.

All this does not prove that either assimilation or multiculturalism is the better way, but it does suggest that assimilation is the safer way.

Perpetuating Multiculturism

Many reasons can be found for minorities to favor multiculturism over assimilation and seek to perpetuate it.

It is easy and temping to presume that a minority person prefers the way of life of their immigrant ancestors even though those ancestors could be three or more generations removed from them. They never personally experienced the historic cultural environment that existed in the old country, yet they could be wrapping themselves in the flag of the old country.

Perhaps they gave thought to what they do and actually believe in the old ways, but it is more likely that they routinely honor the ways and beliefs of their fathers. It is a natural thing to do, definitely not unnatural. Whether they realize it or not, by merely being in America and being exposed to the mainstream culture, learning the language, watching TV, using social media, and perhaps going to school here, the process of assimilation has begun. Once again, it is natural, definitely not unnatural.

Over time, perhaps by the third or fourth generation, use of the old language disappears and the old ways fall by the wayside. However, the mainstream culture is still around and has become more encompassing, and the assimilation process continues. Once again, it is natural, definitely not unnatural.

Thus, although assimilation doesn't necessarily start as a deliberative process, the process naturally and normally leads towards assimilation. As assimilation does not require the dumping of the ways and beliefs of the old culture, and as the brain is not emptied and the mind cleared, parts of the old cultures survive in mainstream society while the old cultural group as such disappears in time.

This must be known to the die-hards and leaders of the old cultural groups who have a vested interest in their groups surviving, perhaps based on merely liking what they have. Some might have a financial interest in preserving what they have.

The disappearance of an old cultural group is against the interests of multiculturalism, which would naturally favor the continued existence of all its constituent members. So the multiculturalists would also have a vested interest in the survival of all cultures as living and vibrant minority groups within their fold. In turn, the minority groups that have survived would naturally try to perpetuate multiculturism that kept it alive and vibrant. This may be so even though there is nothing concrete to show that the minority groups actually help one another.

It is only the assimilated from minority groups who don't have a vested interest in keeping the old cultural group alive and vibrant. Those who left the minority group recently, while the old beliefs and ways are still strongly in their minds, know that they can keep the selected beliefs and ways even though the cultural group is no long theirs. Those who left the group some time ago might not even recognize how their old group evolved over the years and could not care whether the group survives as memories of old beliefs and ways long ago faded away.

So society winds up with opposing camps when it comes to perpetuating old minority cultural groups. One camp is intensely interested in perpetuating the existence of the old cultural group and the other camp is indifferent to its continued existence to various degrees.

The intensely interested is normally likely to overwhelm the largely indifferent, so the public sees and hears much from the multiculturalists about the desirability and need to preserve all cultural groups and sees and hears little that diminishes the need for a groups continued existence. It's the way of the world, those with a voice and commitment get heard.

Recent decades have seen the advent of different reasons for immigrating to America. Initially it was refugee immigrants who sought to escape harm and perhaps death in the old country where they faced officially sanctioned discrimination and physical abuse. They sought freedom and when they got to America, they achieved that whether they stayed huddled in their minority group or assimilated. They would have no apparent reason to support or reject multiculturalism or its perpetuation.

Later, the rationale for immigrating to America largely became escaping poverty and improving their standard of living. Assimilation would better serve that purpose, although the new immigrant might not focus on this. The sophisticated multiculturists are focused and would recognize that the immigrants basically came to America to assimilate and improve their standard of living.

In the situation, the multiculturists had to and did work even harder to curtail assimilation. Perhaps the new immigrants and their leaders weren't sophisticated enough to realize that the multiculturalists were not their friends and that the multiculturalists actually opposed what they intended to do upon immigrating.

Alternatively, perhaps it could be said that the immigrants pride in their culture induced them to agree with the multiculturalists approach that separation from mainstream society would best enhance and perpetuate their culture and that comes first.

But then again, how much pride could the immigrants have had in their old culture that kept them in poverty with a low enough standard of living to cause them to leave that country? Such a minority group supporting multiculturism and it perpetuation could merely be based on being fed misinformation, since assimilation would allow them to perpetuate the features of the culture they want preserved, but not living in hut and kowtowing to the tribal leader.

A new tactic appears to have been adopted by a number, hopefully few, of recent immigrants who did not come to America to adopt a new country but rather immigrated in order to attempt to change American attitudes to the old country and convert Americans to their cause.

Their apparent goal was to obtain political power and use it to propagandize Americans. They don't give fig for America, nor for the many other minority groups they rub against. They weren't interested in building a better future for everybody, but were interested what they can do for their compatriots and their cause. They too would have no apparent reason to support or reject multiculturalism or its perpetuation, other than as cover for what they do.

Discriminating Against Minority Groups

As in any large society, there are people of all attitudes and ideologies. Some are just tribal and only trust and relate to members of their present tribe (Americans) and members of their former tribe (ethnic preference). They might also be intensely nationalistic (loyalty to your nation outweighs everything else) and not merely patriotic (devotion, loyalty to your nation). Others dislike, distrust, fear, or are plain prejudiced against people from other countries (xenophobic). Others consider themselves to be elite and are prejudiced against the poor or those who live in squalor (class-conscious).

But it cannot be said that mainstream Americans normally discriminate against minority groups because of such views. America today has and for decades had a host of programs to help the poor and help families cope with life, minority groups included. All a person need do is delve into the Federal, state and city budgets to identify such programs and the amounts spent on them to prove that the minority groups are being helped, not discriminated against. Accusations by multiculturalists that the mainstream majority deliberately passes legislation to disadvantage minorities is just malarkey because the record shows only equal treatment and focused help when needed.

With mainstream society working to combat many problems facing America and its minority groups, some minority leaders could view mainstream successes as diminishing their value, importance, and status as leaders. After all, some minority leaders actively and openly oppose the mainstream majority, as shown by their emphasis on differentiation and separation. So the multiculturalists are there to undermine mainstream America. It is not that mainstream America discriminates against or undermines minority groups.

Now enter the Russians, or other nations hostile to America, using their cyber-craft to support and create ever more disagreements, strife and conflict within America so as to diminish America itself. What better way is there to destroy a nation, considering that **a house divided against itself cannot stand**, as Abraham Lincoln had said.

Action on all of these fronts (eliminating poverty, supporting family/parental guidance, countering internal conflicts and countering the Russians) should be priorities for mainstream

America and justification for devoting human resources and treasure to these efforts.

Dangers Presented by Multiculturalism

One of the dangers of a multicultural society as America presently has is that one cultural group might attack another cultural group or attack the mainstream group. Right now, there is only the prospect of verbal wars. If and when the verbal wars accelerate beyond the wishes of the activists, matters could easily spin out of control. Should extremists on either side get involved, street conflicts become conceivable. Of course, America provides freedom of speech, so America is hamstrung in containing the verbal conflict that can lead to actual conflict where people are physically hurt.

Consider what did happen recently to illustrate the point being made. Rashida Tliab of Detroit Michigan was elected as the first Palestinian-American Congresswoman. When she won her Democrat primary, she was photographed celebrating while wrapped in a large Palestinian flag, setting the stage for what was to come.

It came right after she took her seat in January 2019 when she accused Republican Senators voting on a bill dealing with a boycott of Israel of "forgetting what country they represent." The American Constitution would protect her freedom of speech even should she verbally becomes more passionately anti-Israel, which she has every right to do. Turn-about by questioning her about what country she represents would be fair game, but unnecessary considering her flag-wrapping.

The point here is only that this is exactly what the Melting Pot was created to stop. Remember this from *The Melting Pot* play:

> "A fig for your feuds and vendettas! Germans and Frenchmen, Irishmen and Englishmen, Jews and Russians—into the Crucible with you all! God is making the American."

The danger presented by multiculturalism is that it can lead to the animosities existing around the world finding a home in America and tearing America apart. The Melting Pot was a plea to keep your ethnicity, your beliefs and religions but in America submerge them in becoming an American first and foremost.

Some would say that the diversity created by multiculturalism strengthens the nation with the variety of intellects, talents and skills its people have. This is a false argument since those intellects, talents and skills reside in the people themselves, not in the cultural units, and would also strengthen the nation if those people assimilated into mainstream America.

Simply put, a multitude of distinct, separate groups tends to divide and thus weaken a nation. This division of America into separate groups contradicts the motto of America which is" E Pluribus Unum" adopted back in the 18th century. In Latin, it means "out of the many, one." There is no doubt from this that America favors assimilation as the motto was adopted way back in the 18th century when the Constitution was just crafted.

Multiculturalism can take on a very unusual form as shown by the Congressional Prayer Caucus (CPC), a religious right group of legislators actually holding seats in the American Congress taking issue with calling "E Pluribus Unum" the motto of America.

CPC said the motto of America is "In God We Trust" adopted in 1956 when the godless communist witch-hunts were going on in Congress. This newly adopted motto now appears on U.S. coin and currency and in abbreviated form in the national anthem.

Thus, the CPC group is effectively separating itself from the American mainstream and treating itself a separate cultural group dividing America by religion. The group faces off against the freedom of religion cornerstone in the founding of America by insisting on imposing its religion on all Americans. Other members of their religion would agree with the motto "E Pluribus Unum," and not deny its very existence. The CPC believers have essentially become a separate cultural group, separating Americans from one another and harming America.

Since multicultural units can literally feud with each other like the proverbial feuding Hatfields & McCoys, multiculturalism presents a distinct danger to the nation. When Abraham Lincoln said "**A house divided against itself cannot stand.**" he referred to America not being able to last half slave and half free, although he also said that he did not expect the house to fall, but become one thing or another.

Thus, if multiculturalism should become the thing, America would be Balkanized into many separate houses and no longer be recognizable. If assimilation should become the thing, America would revert to being one recognizable house doing what it does.

Be this as it may, such a feud is particularly dangerous to America these days as foreign nations (e.g., Russia) use social media and other tools to intensify or create dissatisfaction within America, chiefly by targeting minority groups and promoting separatism.

Integration without Assimilation

When I first heard of "integration without assimilation" I assumed integration referred to minority groups working together (politically, administratively, economically etc) but retaining their different cultures and not merging into one. My assumption was wrong.

The term "integration" is used in the sense of an individual being accepted into the majority group as an equal whatever her or his heritage, traditions, beliefs and values are, even if they clash with that of the majority group. The nation would be required to offer voting citizenship to the integrated, something that that the assimilated mainstream is unlikely to agree with. Going to the extreme, integration today could accept and naturalize confirmed Nazi.

If the individual or cadres of individuals being integrated believe in slavery, discrimination against women, have their own laws, use violence etc, as they might, and they are being given equal voting rights, there is the possibility that the very fabric of the "integrated" mainstream society can change. This might well lead to violence within the community.

In the American Melting Pot assimilated society such persons couldn't be viewed as assimilated. They wouldn't be viewed as fitting-in. However, I couldn't locate any issue ever being raised about such an individual taking the citizenship Oath of Allegiance in good-faith; that is "bearing true faith" to the Constitution and laws of the United States. Perhaps the issue was never drawn. Or perhaps the Oath, when taken, is never questioned.

Inferiority, Superiority, and Self-Identity

Some observers of the multicultural scene make much about how a minority person's self-identity erodes as her or his group is discriminated against or becomes the target of violence.

Some are said to be ashamed at how other members of their minority group act, dress or live.

Some are even said to develop a self-hatred of themselves or their minority group because of what others might believe of them.

Some try to become invisible, hiding their identity as a member of the group to the extent possible.

On the positive side, a person's minority group could be viewed as being superior to other groups leading to self-identity uplifting. For instance, the minority members could take comfort in maintaining that their group is beautiful, maintaining they are the believers in the true God, or maintaining they can jump higher or run faster than anybody else.

It is not necessarily so that one minority group is inferior or superior to another. They are just different. All groups have their pluses and minuses, some real and some made-up. The positive could be a matter of pride and the negative covered up so as to guard against the devil. Think too much of yourself and evil might befall you, so a better position is to make believe you think little of yourself.

And so forth, as we tip-toe through this wonderland of arguments and positions largely created by those who benefit from it.

Who benefits? The multiculturalists and the single-minded who extoll their minority group above others benefit. Their benefit would be in terms of group status, respect, and a feeling of doing the right thing for their group, and might also be in financial terms (e.g., keeping one's job) or in terms of satisfying the urge for power.

Or it can just be dumb stuff, like hating the smartest kid in the class or the adult version of ridiculing an idea that was not thought of by someone in your group.

This is fertile ground for psychiatrists, psychologists, social scientists, behaviorists and other professionals. Assimilated Americans who don't have a professional or monetary interest in any of this may just feel it can't be a serious enough problem to command much time and attention. Yet it can lead to self-examination as it did with me.

In writing this book, I began to search my mind as to my self-identity in terms of whether I can rightfully be considered a racist because I felt comfortable in marrying within my "tribe." I'm not sure I actively sought to do so, but I might have subconsciously. Perhaps most of society does this, but some people would call that racist.

Yet, I feel that I can and do relate favorably to anyone of any race, creed, or religion. I never even considered living only in a tribal neighborhood. I always chose to live where I wanted to live, but I would have probably avoided living in a neighborhood if I felt I wouldn't fit-in that neighborhood.

I respect all cultures and I could agree that every culture is worth preserving, although I'm not too sure about a couple of brutal cultures that killed their own people.

I don't consider myself to be a racist, and my self-identity remains intact or so I think. I can't really identify my self-identity, I'm just me.

Perhaps I think the way I do because I am assimilated or consider myself assimilated. I suspect that some of the unassimilated individuals in a minority group have a tough time dealing with multiculturalism, particularly if their activists/leaders require extreme differentiation in their "Politics of Difference." What happens to these individuals if they don't want to adopt the required differentiation?

Are they to be ostracized or otherwise punished by the group? Or forced to comply? As immigrants, or children of immigrants, they came to America for freedom and a new life, and here they are being forced ever more into the old way of life and they have to bear group regimentation instead of achieving the freedom they sought. The personal toll on such individuals who wind up in a lock-step group must be great.

Logic indicates that there has to be a range of opinion and outlooks in every group, including minority groups. To believe otherwise effectively serves to acknowledge that regimentation exists within that group. These activists leaders would be practicing exactly what they accuse mainstream society of doing: that is, forcing their adherents to march in lock-step.

Yet, "diversity" is ordinarily a mantra of these activist leaders. They applaud the diverse multicultural groups, but would not stand for any diversity within their group.

The danger of conflict always existed between cultures. History has shown that wars were the rule rather than the exception. This is more easily recognized if we were to refer to tribes rather than cultures although they are essentially the same thing. Tribes are known to fight each other, less so with entire cultures. Tribes and cultures can be friends today and enemies tomorrow, but not so with an assimilated mainstream society having gone through the Melting Pot.

Assimilation is not a mere amalgamation of the constituent parts or the acceptance of the mainstream attributes, but results in a mish-mash that might be richer or poorer. The best and brightest could rise to the top, or be oppressed by the lesser if they are at the top, but all are better off than when they had faced more brutal and widespread oppression.

Multiculturalism makes for oppression, oppression of people within the separate cultural groups. Multiculturalists force separation by maximizing differences within the minority groups. That is forced on the group which is basically oppression. Even if an individual is permitted to stick to what presently exists and not maximize differences, the individual stands out and is stigmatized; which is another form of oppression. The Melting Pot and assimilation is a far better alternative for preserving a person's self-identity.

Decline and Prospective Fall

The trend to multiculturalism increased over the decades as immigration increased. The language barrier and strangeness of the new land must have been scary to the new immigrants, so they tended at first to stick together in the new land. Once a conclave was formed, newer immigrants joined in building it into a cultural community, or a ghetto if they were poor. Those communities or ghettos tended to grow for a while as new immigrants came, and then diminish as members started to assimilate into mainstream society.

Perhaps it took a generation or two, even as much as three or four, for the old language to be lost or fall into disuse. America's refusal to adopt an official language served to deter or defer assimilation, but immigrant education and the passage of time served to diminish use of the separatist foreign languages. At the same time, the immigrants were exposed to the mainstream way of life due to TV, ease of transportation, outside jobs, and a host of other influences, in particular social media.

Logic tells us that individual members of a minority group, left to their own devises, would become more comfortable with the nearby mainstream society over time. Or at least until their leaders started to promote separation. Many members obviously bought into separation while others wouldn't. Some leaders adopted the lock-step regimentation, while they blast the mainstream majority with that accusation.

The minority groups could actually lack cohesion and split internally, but the leaders would never make that known. And those members of the minority group who wouldn't buy into separatism, that is those individuals who feel that separatism is undesirable or diverts time and attention away from worthwhile efforts, would naturally tend to remain silent.

As some members of minority groups did assimilate and leave the minority community, new immigrants of the same ethnicity moved in. Depending on the numbers, the minority group community grew, stayed about the same, or shrank. If the latter, rents probably dropped and some outsiders moved into the community. This unwanted community integration could, in turn, induce more members of the community to leave and assimilate into the mainstream if they could possibly do so.

Whether such "normal" progression can take place as I describe would depend on the leadership of the minority group. Leaders have a vested interest in maintaining the minority under their control, whether religious or secular. And some may need the perpetuation of the minority group as their personal political platform. Striving for power and influence exists in minority groups as it does in mainstream society.

Current predictions are that America will begin to fall apart because of racial discrimination in about the middle of the 21st century as the colored population starts to exceed the white population. However, in my view, racial discrimination by the mainstream population is gone; it having become a thing of the past since the election of President Obama. Statisticians shouldn't continue to keep score by the color of one's skin. It's become irrelevant.

But discrimination continues and is now directed against other things, like perhaps the unwashed, the uncouth or the dangerous in minority groups. Assimilated individuals formerly of a minority group might feel the same way as their mainstream brethren and could wind-up discriminating against segments of their own former group.

Thus, the statistical experts who projected the colored verses white population and forecasted strife merely based on color, measured the wrong thing. In forecasting strife, they should have measured attitudes, which, of course, is difficult if not impossible to do. But, maybe, it's something the pollsters could undertake.

Perhaps forecasters could find a way count the number of people of color who have assimilated into mainstream society and include them statistically as if they were part of the "white" population. That could put-off the trigger date for racial strife in America, if not reverse it if the assimilated have grown more than the minority groups.

Since such a count would also be difficult if not impossible, perhaps the statisticians should just forget about forecasting strife. Statistically counting Coloreds vs Whites no longer has any use or meaning since the surrounding circumstances have changed, particularly the election of President Obama and the expansion of people of color throughout mainstream society, as on TV and at the top of many professions.

In my opinion, multiculturism will lose its status in America, either because it'll become irrelevant or it's done its job. Separatism has become counterproductive in this age of individual excellence, as shown by many in minority groups rising to new heights. To illustrate, I searched my mind for African-Americans of excellence that I happen to know of or somehow learned of during my many years. I included them in my personal listing below of Black excellence in important fields of activity. I am sure a reader's list will differ in many ways since there are so many to choose from:

For excellence in leadership, I thought of Martin Luther
King, Jr. and Oprah Winfrey;
in politics, Barack Hussein Obama II and
Colin Powell;
in acting, Whoopi Goldberg and Morgan
Freeman;
in music, Louis Armstrong and Scott Joplin,
in song, Marian Anderson and Michael
Jackson;
in dance; Judith Jamison and Bill
"Bogangles" Robinson;
in science, George Washington Carver and
Ronald McNair;
in sports, Jesse Owens and Serena Williams.

Not all live today. Notice that all are home grown, and all were or are assimilated.

Then I did some research, unrelated to their field of excellence, as to the things that these people of excellence did or other things about them that were somewhat different so as to get some sense about how broad the African-American community is. This list follows, with there being only one person who was not unusual other than the excellence exhibited in the role the person played:

> Academy Award winner, astronaut, billionaire, born into slavery, community organizer, fine-dining restaurant owner, four star general, National Medal of Arts winner, ordained, posed in swimsuits, Presidential Humanitarian Award winner, Presidential Medal of Freedom winner, railroad worker parents, school drop-out, sharecropper parents.

Notice how broad this is, and also consider that African-American youths are presently cutting new ground in many fields.

Even in face of such excellence exhibited by African-Americans, multiculturalists insisting on maximizing group differences and advocating separation just doesn't make sense any longer.

Differentiation and separation suppresses advancement and oppresses personal freedom while the decades of mainstream assistance, special programs and personal freedom have already elevated the people and allowed excellence to breed.   The facts show that mainstream assimilation works.

It is time for multiculturalism and its multiculturist activists to fade away and start joining the crowd.

Educating Immigrants

The dichotomy between Melting Pot assimilation and multiculturalism carries over to the education of immigrants. Educating immigrants using "American" teaching methodologies accelerates the path to the assimilation of immigrants into mainstream American culture. Educating immigrants using old cultural methodologies bolsters multiculturism and slows the path to assimilation.

The ever continuing and pervasive battle between assimilation and multiculturism, discussed in excruciating detail in other chapters, is just noted here as being a factor in the education of immigrants. It is put aside as attention is directed elsewhere.

Although America has no official language, education in the English language plays an outsized role in the education of immigrants. Some proficiency in English is required for immigrant adults to be naturalized as citizens if that is their goal. It is also required on a day-to-day basis to drive and read traffic signs, useful in using public transportation, useful in reading store signs and official notices and a host of other lifestyle matters. And the education of adults is vastly different from the way children are educated.

Adults may attempt to rely mostly on the mother tongue, while the children are on a path to bilingualism. Counterintuitively, education professionals of all types seem to agree that children who continue using the mother tongue learn English better and faster than children who attempt the dump the old tongue as soon as possible. Thus first generation bilingualism should be encouraged as helping the children, and also helping their parents as the children become interpreters for the family.

Things become difficult for the teachers as they have to cope with the different styles of education abroad, which depend on the cultural traditions of the parents, like learning by rote in some societies, the use of flashcards in others, concentration on dry subject matter rather than using childhood storybooks etc. And there is the problem of dealing with strict, liberal or uncaring parents.

In addition, the overburdened teachers have to deal with the ever changing basic approaches to American education; one approach emphasizing one subject matter or another from time to time as society advances, and the other approach that consistently emphasizes a more open educational style that could foster thinking and innovation.

Education of teachers also varies, with most of these problem areas probably covered. Nevertheless, education appears to be a very difficult subject matter, aside from having to deal with the assimilationists and the multiculturists attempting to use education as one of their tools.

Some Legal Requirements

As with all children in America, the children of immigrants are required to be educated either in the public schools, in state-certified private schools or in approved home education programs. Both legal and illegal (undocumented) immigrant children must be educated due to the 1982 Supreme Court decision in Plyler v. Doe. That case's coverage of illegal immigrants was changed in some ways by a 1996 statute passed by Congress, but still has broad application.

The 1974 Supreme Court decision in Lau v. Nichols, based on the Civil Rights Act, held that the school districts receiving federal funds must provide special language assistance programs to students who do not speak English or are deficient in it.

 In this back-door way, English proficiency became required through much of America even though America has no official language. Federal funds accounts for about 8% of the total funds spent in America on Kindergarten to 12th grade (K-2) education, most of which is earmarked for specific programs. I could find no statistics on the percentage of K-12 schools these funds reach.

In such cases where English must be taught, the teachers must be competent in the languages used by their immigrant students.

Beyond secondary public school education, there is no Federal requirement that the states provide college level education or any other type of education (e.g., job or skills education) to any of its residents, including legal and illegal immigrants. Nor is there any Federal law barring such education or barring legal or illegal immigrants from attending. All that is left to the states, and immigrants being able to afford it or the state providing financial assistance.

Curriculums of Private Schools

At first blush, it might seem that a state should not be involved in what private schools teach. However, states have a mandate to assure that all children residing in the state get a basic education and the state has the power to force students to attend a school that provides the basic education.

This doesn't require the state to force children to attend public schools, but rather the state must assure that a child receive a basic education from whatever school the child attends, whether it be public or private, parochial or secular schools, or even home education.

Thus, if a private school fails to provide the minimum basic education, the state would have the right to force the private school to provide the courses needed to comply with minimum basic education. As a result, the state actually has the obligation to get involved in the curriculum of private schools even though it might at first appear that the state is interfering in private matters.

Use of the English Language

As previously stated, under the 1974 Supreme Court decision, school districts receiving federal funds have to provide English language programs for students not proficient in English.

If a state should require that every child learn the English language, all K-12 schools in the state, including minority cultural schools fighting assimilation, would have to include English language courses in their curriculums. The state has its traffic signs in English and communicates in many ways with its residents in the English language. A group not knowing the English language creates dangers for the group as well as dangers for the community.

Instead, should the state decide to have two official languages so as to help a large segment of its population, it could mandate that either language be taught in all schools. Traffic signs and other state communications would still have to be in English for most of the State, perhaps with exceptions in local areas where a single foreign language dominates. Or, everything might be in dual languages. Either way, this adds additional expense to the State budget and doesn't satisfy everyone since other groups would be left out.

Actually, the duel language approach would be a form of state or official discrimination (as everyone is not treated equally), and an expensive one at that. As much as a group might want to keep to themselves and use only their own language, they have no right to dictate what the State might or might not do. If they are citizens, they can vote like everyone else in the State, but not dictate.

From the Melting Pot point of view, some degree of assimilation should be expected in every group that makes up our multicultural nation. There should be no discrimination in the state's minimum basic education requirements, with no school of any type being required to do more or less than other types of schools.

While the Federal government has not adopted English as the official language, proficiency in English has been made a requirement in the naturalization process for American citizenship.

Affirmative action in college education worked in practice. It did create educational opportunities for Blacks that wasn't otherwise available to them, and also for some Latino-Americans.

 The other side of the affirmative action coin is that favoring one group, no matter how justifiable, must of necessity discriminate against others. With a Black having been elected President of America showing how much Blacks have advanced and assimilated, it may again or soon be time to adopt an admission process based strictly on merit and seeking excellence.

Everybody should benefit from this as excellence is need more than ever for America to compete in the world markets, and the better America does at this, the more every person in America benefits.

Literacy Learning Practices

Different countries have different styles, methods and approaches in classroom and content education. Of course, the age of the student body is primary. American teachers should understand the literacy learning practices of immigrants and minority students they happen to face in the classroom. For instance, the primary learning practice could be education by rote (repetition and memorization). In another country, students might use flash cards or other props. Some use storybooks, others don't. Some emphasize math, others science, and so forth.

Teachers in classrooms full of recent immigrants to America need to understand the literacy learning practices prevalent in the counties of origin and how to deal with it in the American classroom.

Time, effort and treasure would be well spent on training teachers to understand and deal with these cultural differences, on whether they should accept the foreign way to some extent or substitute the American way, and to determine how to duck the slings and arrows of the assimilationists and multiculturalists. Yes, every effort to use the American way will be applauded by the assimilationists and condemned by the multiculturalists, and visa-versa.

Administrators have it somewhat easier in the sense that they only have to deal with content, and as to that they have been vastly criticized for underemphasizing mathematics. America scored badly in international rankings of math education, but there is another side to that story, which follows.

Educating for Innovation

A favorite author of mine, Fareed Zakaria, in his book *In Defense of a LIBERAL EDUCATION* published in 2015, promotes a liberal education over a skill-based education. In doing so he pointed out that America, Sweden and Israel all do miserably in education excellence measurements as compared to other nations. For instance, the three are very low in their mathematics rankings which, in America, led to panic drives to improve math education.

Yet, Zakaria points out that these three nations lead the world in innovation, including scientific innovation that uses mathematics. So what gives? In America, it seems to be the broad scope of the classes offered students and their freedom to pick and choose for themselves (instead of having detailed mandated requirements) that tend to lead to innovation. This is one of the advantages of the liberal education, American style.

A Korean Educational Story and the American Melting Pot

An extraordinary human-interest story just hit the press in South Korea that indirectly highlights what the American Melting Pot might bring to the educational table. A 2019 article written by the Jewish Telegraphic Agency describes how study-crazy South Korea seized on the Jewish Talmudic tradition as the way to improve their educational system. Unrecognized as such or called by another name, the same tradition can be found in the higher level liberal education in America.

The South Koreans were flabbergasted by what the Jews achieved:

> " 'Jews account for just 0.2 percent of the world's population, but 23 percent of Nobel Prize winners have been Jewish,' Seoul-based student Choi Jae-young related. 'And despite all the time and money we spend on education, only one Korean has ever won a Nobel award. That irks many Koreans. It makes us want to learn Jews' secrets.' "

98

Rabbi Marvin Tokayer, a chaplain with the American military, wrote about the Talmud, which had gone viral after it hit South Korean bookstores. What the South Koreans learned was that the Talmudic scholars had students pair off to debate one another, asking and responding to questions. Doing this apparently forced the student to really understand what they were dealing with, a far cry from the South Korean practice of just memorizing what they read or were told.

Nobody had to learn Hebrew and Aramaic in which the Talmud was written or study why the rabbis themselves argued so much:

> " 'Koreans don't have to emulate Jewish belief systems,' educational researcher Seol Dong-ju said, 'but we do need to copy the way Jews teach their children.' "

Jewish assimilation into mainstream American society may have indirectly brought the Talmudic tradition of open disagreement and debate into the American universities, particularly those providing a liberal education, and some of it must have found its way in family home life.

I can personally testify to such untaught use in family home life as I witnessed the dinner table debates between my grandchildren and their parents as to weighty matters like taking out the garbage. I was amazed as to how many arguments could be dredged up in those duels. So perhaps it just arises naturally when people discuss or argue things.

THE MELTING POT

Immigration Policy

The political and business aspects of present day immigration drives America's immigration policy or, more precisely, drives America's inability to agree on an immigration policy.

On the political side of immigration policy, it is relatively clear that the most recent immigrants to America, namely Hispanic-Americans (including Latinos and Chicanos), vote Democratic.

In a November 8, 2018 article, the Pew Research Center estimated that 69% of Hispanics voted Democratic and 29% voted Republican in the nationwide 2018 mid-term congressional elections. Hispanics make up 30% of eligible voters in Texas, with 64% of the Hispanics voting Democratic and 35% Republican in the Senate race and 53% vs 42% in the race for governor.

Using the honored law-enforcement practice of exploring **"who benefits?"** more from immigration, it's clear that Democrats benefit politically. From this, a person might reasonably conclude that the Democrats are all for continued high immigration.

In terms of the business side of immigration policy, business people in both the Republican and Democratic camps would benefit from the lower wages paid immigrants so many business people would favor more immigration. A few business people might complain about the low immigrant-wages paid by their business competitors, but this has to be insignificant. Without getting into a debate about whether more business people are Republicans or Democrats, let's merely say that both Democratic and Republican business people could benefit from high immigration.

Thus, from the business viewpoint, both Democrats and Republicans benefit from high immigration. But from the political viewpoint, only the Democrats benefit politically from high immigration and will probably benefit more in the future as ever more Hispanic immigrants become voting citizens.

However, there is no cohesion amongst Democrats or amongst Republicans, for there are many in both political parties that believe the national interest, however they define it, comes first. Sadly, there are too few of them. And there are more than enough intransigent members of Congress, both Republicans and Democrats, who would block any legislation on immigration policy order to maintain the status quo.

Unrestricted & Legally Restricted Entry

When groups of thousands of would-be immigrants are observed marching from afar to get into America, some Americans cheer at their commitment and bravery, while other Americans feel that nobody has a right to just get up and move to America.

Yet, America is a nation of immigrants, except for the Native Americans, immigrants who built a wonderful place to live over the centuries. This success provided more reason for more people to immigrate to America. But being a nation of immigrants does not necessarily mean that America should forever be barred from restricting immigration and restrictions were legally mandated by Congress over time.

When America first became a nation, there were no laws restricting immigration. Anyone could come in any number. Over time, America found it necessary to limit immigration. The Page Act of 1875 and the Chinese Exclusion Act of 1882 started off with the exclusion of so-called "undesirable" aliens [undefined] and ended with immigration limitations on Chinese laborers. At that time it was the American wage earners who complained that the low wages of the Chinese brought their wages down.

The Immigration Act of 1924 started the numerical limitation on immigrants, a quota system mostly directed at non-European immigrants. Although it reflected racial discrimination as did the previous legislation, it was an official declaration that too many immigrants were entering America. The 1952 Immigration and Nationality Act continued the quota system and added skill based quotas, so as to fill America's need for certain talented people. Fears of ordinary immigrants going on welfare and taking jobs from persons born in Americans were heard at that time. Along the way, seasonal agricultural workers from Mexico were temporarily admitted to fill agricultural-labor shortages.

In 1965 the immigration laws were amended to drop the national quotas, but it did add the first quota on Western Hemisphere immigration into America. It also added a unification procedure for family members and skilled immigrants.

The unification provision later grew into a major pathway to increased immigration into America because a child born in America would be an American citizen, whether born of temporary or illegal immigrants, even those who were later booted out of America. When grown-up, the child could bring close and remote family members into America. This made for exponential immigration growth.

As a relevant digression, along the way American big-business convinced Congress to create the special H-1B visa for "high-skilled" technical, scientific and administrative etc personnel that couldn't be filed by Americans because they didn't have the skills. About 150,000 of such "high-skilled" workers were entering America annually with H-1B visas.

The L-1 visas allowed multinational American companies to transfer from their foreign operations skilled managers and other such workers to America because Americans with such skills couldn't be found, and about 150,000 of such manager/worker entered America annually.

At the rate of 300,000 a year, millions of American jobs were lost to H-1B and L-1 visa holders in very little time. Perhaps this is what contributed to or caused the stagnation of middle-class wages in America.

The inability to find Americans with the skills required to fill such jobs had to be proven, which was apparently easy to do in-house (basically, affidavits that you tried and failed), but impossible to disprove by those who issue the visas. Thus another loophole was created, this time to get higher-paid workers into America. Then have a baby born in America, and in a decade or so the entire family can move to America.

From time to time, various groups expressed fears that immigrants would lower American wages, take jobs from native-born Americans or become public charges. The issue was joined by those favoring immigration starting to maintain that Americans did not want to take those lowly jobs and immigrants were needed to full them. But now, higher paid jobs were also going to would-be immigrants through the special visa programs, and high level American workers started to complain.

As a personal aside, I recall the time when Steve Jobs, the famed leader of Apple, harangued President Obama for not admitting more skilled foreign engineers, scientists and technicians into America because American colleges and universities were not graduating enough of the skilled for him to hire. I also recall my reaction to this, which was that American schools had the ability to educate and graduate enough of the necessary skilled workers if Steve Jobs had the jobs for them in America instead of building his plants abroad or getting foreign companies to manufacture his products.

But in the end, all this detail faded into the background as illegal immigration grew exponentially. Aside from the various laws passed by Congress reflecting the basic American view that there should be limitations on immigration, some of those laws changed the status of aliens already here legally. That actually led to more illegal immigration as the newly barred aliens found ways to illegally enter America but the numbers are probably insignificant considering the magnitude of the immigration problem.

Logic tells us that unlimited immigration cannot go on forever. America is such a desirable place to live that a good portion of the world's needy would want to live here. And because America is a safe place to live and protect assets, the rich are now flocking to America, primarily from Asia -- but I assume in much lesser numbers than the poor. Simply ball-parking trends, I would say that there are just so many rich who seek safety and asset protection, but many-fold more poor all over the world.

Even if millions of the poor were accepted as immigrants into America each year, the growth of poverty abroad is much faster and more and more immigrants would have to be accepted into America annually and still not catch up with the poverty growth abroad.

As is being heard today, taking the skilled [e.g., doctors] from such nations, and supplying our skilled [e.g., doctors] to help those nations, is not a logical way to help. If anything, our immigration policy should be geared to not accepting the skilled, middle-class immigrants from poor countries so that they would remain abroad and hopefully build their own nation, providing jobs and revenues to educate their poor.

Perhaps we can also get American business owners, corporate executives, venture capitalists and philanthropists to help the needy abroad by developing and funding entrepreneurial ventures abroad that provide jobs now, and will present growth opportunities for the poor in the future.

America economically helping the impoverished nations develop would be the better way to serve the poor of those nations and probably be less costly to America than dealing with and caring for the immigrants. It is also within the power of the American government to provide such entrepreneurial ventures as indicated above, gratis or with pay-back in time.

Starting to ween those poor countries away from cash and material support and starting to sponsor entrepreneurial projects that employ locals makes sense. However, that will probably be blocked politically by those politicians who want immigration growth because the immigrants are expected to eventually vote for them and/or work for their business constituents.

This is clearly a dismal forecast, but a justifiable one considering the current inability of our legislators to agree on anything meaningful concerning immigration.

Legal Turning into Illegal Immigration

A legal immigrant is a person authorized to live and work in America on a permanent basis. These people are the green-card holders who passed muster at the border. Asylum seekers can also become permanent residents, as can others qualifying under a variety of special programs.

America also has wonderful visa laws allowing aliens to enter America for various non-immigration, temporary purposes, like touring, visiting family or friends, going to school, attending business meetings, etc. However, some of these visa holders take jobs in America, when their admission doesn't allow it. Other visa holders don't renew their visas and merely disappear into American society in droves. And America appears to be totally unable to enforce the time or other limitations on these visas. In these ways, illegal immigration swells.

Asylum seekers might be denied asylum, as a very large percentage are, and they too might disappear in the American country side. But even before their cases are heard, many just disappear.

So it is not just the illegal border crossers that makes up the illegal immigrant population in America. It might be the visa jumpers who make for the most illegal immigrants.

Merit-Based Immigration

Canada and Australia, two other nations built by immigrants, have gone to a merit-based immigration system. Merit-based immigration entails accepting people of accomplishment, like doctors, scientists, teachers, athletes, musicians, actors or the like. These could be the people of merit America would favor or actually need.

Merit-based immigration sounds good, but it does have a significant downside. It robs poor countries of the meritorious people those counties have, and need to survive and grow. Thus, as the meritorious run to America to improve their living standard, they depress the living standard and potential for growth in their homeland.

Some Americans say that merit-based immigration isn't morally correct or fair and is essentially discriminatory.

Perhaps America should be blind to merit and just adopt some sort of random selection process. Or perhaps America should accept as immigrants the meritorious from countries that can afford to lose them, and not accept the meritorious from backward nations.

This would be official discrimination, but it does smack of being morally correct. Remember, it was considered morally correct for America to have affirmative action programs, and yet that was official discrimination. It is time for America to address and decide this issue along with all the other immigration issues.

Asylum for Refugees

As a sovereign nation, America could enact its own laws governing the granting of asylum in America to refugees as it defines that term. However, America yielded its sovereignty in this regard in 1968 by ratifying a 1967 United Nations Protocol that amended the "Convention Relating to the Status of Refugees" approved by the United Nations in 1951. Although America ratified the 1967 Protocol, America never specifically ratified the 1951 Convention. It is indeed complicated.

To add to the United Nations complications, America expressly refused to ratify the United Nations treaty creating the International Criminal Court, refusing to be bound by that court as it applied so-called "international law."

There is no written body of international law agreed to by any or many nations. Rather the United Nations considers international law to be what is "customarily" considered to be international law, a rather vague approach. "Customarily" where, when and how determined is left unstated.

As nations could not and would not agree as to what is customary, the United Nations would treat as customary what has not been agreed to. To do so, the United Nations had to resort to treating silence as consent unless specific objections are registered. Forcing specific objections to the vague and treating silence as consent, and away we go into a brave new world. So much for "international law."

Applications for asylum can be filed at a point of entry or while in America. America offers asylum for refugees based on proof of actual persecution or well-grounded fear of persecution based on the applicant's social group, race, religion, nationality, or political opinions. Most asylum applications are denied because they are based on family squabbles leading to physical harm or based on fear of local gangs; neither rising to the needed level of persecution. And there are procedures upon procedures, judges upon judges, appeals and appeals to obtain asylum, a process that could take a year or much more with detention in the meantime.

Asylum applications can be used to game the immigration laws, and that could account for the tremendous increase in asylum applications in recent years. A pending asylum claim allows a couple to have a child born in America, who when grown up would get the family accepted as legal immigrants. Asylum claims can be refiled after denial and deportation. And by being in America, it offer the possibility of an opportunity opening to disappear into America society during the long period of asylum detention. Living as one of the millions of illegal immigrants already in America keeps the dream alive of eventual acceptance.

Immigration Statistics

The "Project Gutenberg" published text of *The Melting Pot* play was accompanied by an appendix that contained a table entitled "ALIENS ADMITTED TO THE UNITED STATES IN THE YEAR ENDED JUNE 30TH, 1913" under the heading "THE MELTING POT IN ACTION."

The source of that table wasn't mentioned, but the use of a June 30th fiscal year indicated it was a U.S. government source because the government uses that fiscal year. The table was for the year 1913, indicating that a table for 1908 when *The Melting Pot* play opened probably wasn't compiled or available. This is what the published 1913 table of immigrants contained:

African (black)	9,734
Armenian	9,554
Bohemian and Moravian	11,852
Bulgarian, Servian, Montenegrin	10,083
Chinese	3,487
Croatian and Slavonian	44,754
Cuban	6,121
Dalmatian, Bosnian, Herzegovinian	4,775
Dutch and Flemish	18,746
East Indian	233
English	100,062
Finnish	14,920
French	26,509

German	101,764
Greek	40,933
Hebrew	105,826
Irish	48,103
Italian (north)	54,171
Italian (south)	264,348
Japanese	11,672
Korean	74
Lithuanian	25,529
Magyar	33,561
Mexican	15,495
Pacific Islander	27
Polish	185,207
Portuguese	14,631
Roumanian	14,780
Russian	58,380
Ruthenian (Russniak)	39,405
Scandinavian	51,650
Scotch	31,434
Slovak	29,094
Spanish	15,017
Spanish-American	3,409
Syrian	10,019
Turkish	2,132
Welsh	3,922
West Indian (except Cuban)	2,302
Other peoples	3,512
Total	1,427,227

In those days, say about 1% of the legal immigrants came from across the Pacific Ocean, a little less than 2% came from South of the border, and the balance crossed the Atlantic Ocean mostly from "white" Europe. Immigration from "African (black)" was less than 1%. Thus, immigration was basically White, making assimilation by surmounting ethnicity through the Melting Pot crucible more foreseeable.

It cannot be said that race prejudice played an official part in determining which aliens were to be admitted. However, the manner in which the immigration statistics were officially presented indicates that race considerations could have played a part in how the immigrants were listed.

However, on Ellis Island where immigrants were actually admitted to America, the emphasis seemed to be on just admitting them, even resorting to making up new names for them when their name were unpronounceable. I have no knowledge as to my mother's real name; she became a "Smith" upon immigration. I also don't know how my father's name became "Lamp."

For instance, listing "African (black)" instead of the countries involved could indicate that officialdom included only Blacks who came from Africa and excluded the Whites from this category. Except possibly for South Africans, there were probably few Whites and many African countries, so officialdom could have merely listed "Africa." To me, it appeared that officialdom was deliberately introducing race.

Jewish immigrants weren't included as coming from their country of source or origin. They were listed as "Hebrew," which is a religion or sometimes considered to be a race. No other immigrants were listed by religion or race. The classification as Hebrew could have reflected an official bias, but more likely the government couldn't figure out how to classify a group that appeared to have no "homeland" since they were scattered throughout Europe.

Italian immigration was broken down into two parts; those from the north and those from south of Italy. On what basis did the government distinguish between Northern and Southern Italians? Perhaps culturally, economic status, or even political. There is no way to determine this.

Country of origin immigration statistics change dramatically since that reported for 1913. According to the Pew Research Center, in 2017 there were almost 50 million people living in the United States who were <u>born in other countries</u>. The number of such immigrants in America by country of origin were (the table shown here was shortened by stopping at 100,000):

Mexico	12,680,000
China	2,420,000
India	2,310,000
Philippines	2,080,000
Puerto Rico	1,900,000
Vietnam	1,410,000
El Salvador	1,390,000
Cuba	1,250,000
South Korea	1,180,000
Dominican Republic	1,070,000
Guatemala	980,000
Canada	890,000
Jamaica	770,000
Colombia	750,000
United Kingdom	750,000
Haiti	670,000
Germany	650,000
Honduras	600,000
Peru	480,000
Poland	470,000
Ecuador	470,000

Russia	420,000
Iran	400,000
Italy	390,000
Ukraine	380,000
Turkey	370,000
Pakistan	370,000
Japan	370,000
Brazil	370,000
Guyana	290,000
Nigeria	280,000
Nicaragua	280,000
Thailand	260,000
Trinidad and Tobago	250,000
Hong Kong	240,000
Venezuela	230,000
Bangladesh	220,000
Ethiopia	220,000
Laos	210,000
Iraq	210,000
Argentina	200,000
Portugal	200,000
Egypt	190,000
France	180,000
Cambodia	180,000
Romania	170,000
Ghana	160,000
Greece	150,000
Israel	140,000
Ireland	140,000
Burma (Myanmar)	130,000
Lebanon	130,000
Bosnia-Herzegovina	130,000
Kenya	120,000

Tunisia	120,000
Panama	110,000
Spain	110,000
Chile	100,000
Nepal	100,000
Indonesia	100,000
South Africa	100,000

90 other countries were omitted as the list continued to go below 100,000 immigrants per country.

Thus, the number of potential ethnicities in America is mind boggling. Imagine how difficult it would be to even recognize a fraction of them or learn how to greet them. Big groups, like those of Hispanic or Asian origin, can be found all over America, with some groups dominating the metropolitan areas they find attractive.

Non-Hispanic Whites and Blacks, who have been in America much longer, are getting older. Both the assimilated Whites and Blacks are giving way to the newer groups. Political power is shifting.

Statistical computations indicate that people of color in America will outnumber the White mainstream at some time in the middle of the 21st century, triggering an age of conflict. However, color discrimination no longer defines America, making such statistics irrelevant.

The Melting Pot has been working and many people of color have assimilated into the mainstream, so the mainstream is no longer very White. If the assimilated and non-assimilated were able to be counted, the statistics would be very different and probably point to no trigger date for conflict.

Notwithstanding all the pressure the multiculturalists are capable of, it does seem that the present age is accelerating Melting Pot assimilation. Unfortunately, American youth do not think about, or are even aware of, these terms and concepts. They should be aware since it's their country at stake.

Dated Justifications for Immigration
Justifications for allowing immigration to America can be dated in the sense that those justifications no longer exist at the time immigration takes place. The justifications, still in the minds of Americans, make it easy to swell the immigration totals. Or possibly, such unjust immigration displaces just immigration.

A relevant tale, on the bright side, appeared in an article written by Yelena Akhtiorskaya and published in The New York Times on Dec. 14, 2018. Yelena immigrated to Brooklyn, NY at the age of 6 from a paradise [as he called it] in Odessa, Russia. The official justification for allowing immigration was based on anti-Semitic persecution even though there were no pogroms, rapes, or pillaging of Jews at that time. There were only some minor discriminations against Jews that in Yelena's view were "trivialities that only a wimp would see as abuse."

Material like this is not to be expected in print, but it does suggest that a variety of biases, preferences, or political issues could drive official immigration decisions from time to time. My favorite culprit is politics.

Attitudes to Immigration

In this age of the internet for information availability, the cellphone for ease of communication, the jet and performance cars for ease of transportation, the pace of change has made it it's difficult to pinpoint current attitudes to immigration and exactly how they changed from a decade or so ago.

Availability of the new lifestyle improvements (or detriments as some people see them) is limited where poverty resides, but some of the improvements leach through. Now those in poverty living abroad are probably more aware of how great it can be living elsewhere; introducing, enhancing or making more urgent the desire to immigrate.

New immigration policies in developed nations, and in particular the European Union, has widened or totally opened the door for immigration and in so doing bolstered the desire and ability of both the poor and many others to emigrate to those lands. The new immigrants came in droves for the available jobs and an improvement in living standards, forming cultural groups or conclaves in the new lands. Some of the old residents praised the newly created diversity and welcomed the new residents and the economic gains they brought forth, while some of old residents bemoaned the changes in the very fabric of their old society.

Within the European Union, the British population voted expressly to exit the Union (called "Brexit") because the Union's rules allowed and forced the fabric change in their society, with the British population at large willing to forgo the economic gains the Union created. When the manner of exiting the Union shifted over to the British parliament, the business interests favoring remaining in the Union became apparent, creating an unusual dysfunctionality in that government. And so the matter stands in Britain.

But pressure elsewhere within the European Union forced to Union to constrict its former immigration policies in order to keep the Union together. There is now a 325 mile border-barrier (solid walls and barbed wire fences) built by the Hungarian military on the borders between Hungary and Serbia/Croatia/Slovenia to stop immigrants and asylum seeks from entering Hungary, a member of the Union. This was Hungary turning around on its former position of accepting asylum seekers and immigrants and being a gateway to entering the rest of the Union.

I suspect that if a vote were taken in the Union today, German Chancellor Angela Merkel's immigration and asylum laws would be repealed by the people in the Union. If so, it would be in stark contrast with the business interests in Germany (the most successful in Europe) which would favor high immigration and the resultant lower wages.

All this shows that a basic split now exists between the general population and business interests, where the people now consider their communities and way of life as being more important than business success. While such a vote in the Union is speculation, it would be confirmed by the British peoples' Brexit vote and the Union's current curtailment of its asylum and immigration policies.

The people's attitude in these developed nations trending to disfavor immigration comes into stark contrast with the increasing desire of poor and other people in less-developed nations increasing desire to emigrate. Perhaps this is now mitigating in that the economic position of the less-developed nations could be improving as the developed world seeks new sources of raw materials or cheap labor to support its growth by developing, financing and building projects in those less developed nations.

Perhaps all this suggests that a reversal in attitudes might be in the works. For instance, as Mexico begins to look better and better economically more Mexicans are beginning to favor remaining in Mexico to immigrating to America, and the Mexican government seems to be accepting as Mexican immigrants people who were crossing their land to get into America and couldn't.

That says nothing about America itself beginning to build walls to block illegal immigration, to the displeasure of those Americans who benefit from it or morally favor immigration on the one hand and those who disfavor immigration.

That's where it stands today, the apparent winner being the people's elevation of social concerns over economic practicalities. This essentially is a blow against immigration and multiculturism. But, then again, much of this is speculation as we just don't know where it will end.

Economic Inequality
Socialism / Communism / Capitalism

It is early 2019 and I have come to believe that the clash between assimilation and multiculturalism has largely played-out. Some of the rhetoric remains but it is going nowhere. It's being replaced by the new issue getting the attention of Congress, a whale of an issue.

That issue revolves around the extraordinary economic inequality in America. By every measure, the economic gulf between the super-elite and the average American has broken through the charts. The statisticians argue amongst themselves as to how to measure the disparity, and are unlikely to ever agree. And that is not where the action is.

Our legislators in Washington DC have started to talk, in and outside the halls of Congress, about their proposals to combat economic inequality. The proposals have been called socialist and communist, but the two are very much the same. For convenience, I'll just use the term socialism.

The socialist proposals in America seem to be going backwards in historical terms as the Chinese and Russian powers had dumped socialism decades ago and had largely gone over to capitalism, American style capitalism. America was gleeful when that happen as it proved that American capitalism was the very best economic system. And both China and Russia have prospered with capitalism.

Briefly put, socialism stands for (A) social welfare for everyone in the nation, with (B) the nation owning the means of production so as to pay for the social welfare.

Well, America does provide some social welfare. America has many programs to foster the social wellbeing of its people, particularly the poor. This has been acceptable to most Americans and it is consistent with Christian principles of charity in this Christian nation. Americans squabble about whether America is doing enough or too much, but in principle America agrees with some degree of social welfare. This is not the primary concern with socialism.

The primary concern is the other part where the nation, the government, owns all the means of production from mining to finished goods, from manufacturing to retailing, from transportation to utilities, including all sorts of service providers and so forth, on and on. That never worked for China and Russia, and they dumped it. They now prosper, particularly in the case of China which had done wonders for its people. The workers in China have enjoyed an unprecedented increase in their standard of living under their new capitalist system while American workers had largely stagnated under its capitalist system.

We all know by now that governments can't run things as efficiently as capitalists can. Since it's the capitalist's money at stake, they watch and manage it with greater care. America did very well with its capitalists running the means of production, making America the richest country in the world. Unfortunately, the capitalists took much too much of the pie. Hence, the huge economic inequality problem America faces. Notwithstanding this, Americans are not likely to accept government ownership of the means of production.

The old socialist nations also had their problems. With workers being promised what they needed, the workers incentive to work disappeared and production efficiency declined materially. The socialists also strove for an economically classless society where everyone was equal, only to find that unbridled corruption and favoritism flourished and created many haves and have nots.

America is founded on equality, equality under the rule of law. That worked, and still works. But the lightest noodle always rises to the top of the soup and at day's end some Americans have much more than others.

Taxation

Oddly enough, many of America's very rich have indicated that an increase in the taxes they pay would be fine with them so as to provide more social welfare, but the greedy amongst them hate to even pay any taxes and use foreign tax havens to evade American taxes.

You could imagine my surprise when I recently sent an opinion piece to one major newspaper after another only to get rejections. I had suggested that America shut down the tax havens by stopping all money transactions between American banks or financial institutions and those nations. Those nations had extended their banking secrecy laws to foreigners, right in America's face, aimed deliberately at harming America by helping greedy Americans evade their taxes. Without the tax havens, the American tax cheats would pay more tax to the US Treasury, and to that extent lessen economic inequality in America in two ways; by reducing the net income of the high-earning tax cheats and by America having more to spend on social welfare.

America has used an arsenal of sanctions against specific nations for specific purposes and they have been proven successful, and it could use anything in its arsenal against the tax havens instead of the one I proposed or in addition to it. But there seems to be too many American lawyers, bankers, and lobbyists who benefit from the existence of the tax havens and are ready to oppose this.

Actually, America can do more to increase tax collections without raising tax rates by upping the budget of the Internal Revenue Service so that the IRS can inforce America's tax laws. Statistics have shown that the IRS collects much, much more in taxes than it spends. But again, the tax greedy in Congress stand against this

Other Suggestions

I had a number of other suggestions to combat economic inequality in America in my books *The Decline and [Preventable] Fall of America* published in 2014, and in *99 Prescriptions for a More Ethical Society* published in 2008.

While we hear some elite American voices welcoming some increase in their taxes, the proposals put on the table by the current activists might appear to be too much, too soon. Yet, we must narrow the economic inequality or our house divided will not stand.

In Conclusion

In conclusion, I favor the Melting Pot and assimilation, as if you didn't know by now.

As I read and reread what I had written, I began to question some of my positions or how I arrived at them. There is nothing like putting positions to paper to make an author think again about what was written. I actually began debating with myself, and only too frequently modified a position.

I do and will always continue to seek what the "other" says, even though it could get me into trouble. When my wife was telling me what was happening in Tibet and what the Dali Lama was saying, I foolishly asked how the Chinese responded to that when I began to fear dinner plates flying at me. And I always try to fairly state the "others" say, without misrepresentation or holding back their arguments.

However, I started to question two major premises of mine, namely to be balanced in my coverage and be politically correct in how I present things. I came to the conclusion that neither would do for an advocate. As I was advocating a position, I should do it forcefully and use all the arguments at hand. Besides, there would be a decent degree of balance because I was also stating the "others" positions and presenting it fairly. And not being politically correct should be okay as long as I was polite in being direct and strive to avoid offending others.

My positions are solely based on logic, reason and honoring the Constitution. No inherited positions are at work, and nothing from my mainstream tribe. Anyone who happens to think like me is my tribe.

And so I feel that all of us of like mind must fight for the soul and continued existence of America by advocating the concept of assimilation, and promoting the ideals behind the Melting Pot.

It is the time to remain civil but openly fight for the Melting Pot as the only means to stem the decline of America and fix our dysfunctional government.

It's time to be outspoken and insist on Melting Pot classes in our universities alongside the multitude of separatist cultural heritage courses. It is time to have the Melting Pot voice heard.

Index

Catholic(s) 25, 44,

Chicano 101,

Chicano-Americans 117,

China(ese) 101, 121, 122,

Chinese Exclusion Act 103,

Christian(s) 10, 11, 120,

Christmas 10,

Citizen(ship) 5, 80, 93, 101,

Civil Right Act 23, 24, 64, 91,

Civil War 22,

Class conscious 75,

Clinton, Hillary 25, 26,

Clinton, William Jefferson 26,

Code of the Street 49, 50,

Coinage 7,

Coloreds 86,

Communist(s)(ism) 8, 14, 65, 78, 121,

Confederacy 22,

Confederation 37,

Conflicts of interests 33, 34,

Congress 5, 12, 19, 36, 52, 91, 104, 105, 121,

Congressional Prayer Caucus 7, 78,

Constitution(a) 5, 8, 9, 11, 19, 35, 39, 77, 78, 126,

Culture(s)(al) 1, etc, etc

Curriculum(s) 91, 92,

Dance 54, 87,

Dated justifications 114,

Declaration of Independance 9, 17, 19,

Declaration of Rights 9,

Democrat(s) 25, 76, 101, 10,

Detroit, MI 76,

Developed nations 115, 117,

Difference(s)(ion) (cultural) 1, 3, 40, 41, 59, 60, 75, 82, 84, 88, 89,

Discriminate(d)(ion)(ing) 47, 48, 57, 58, 74, 80, 85, 86, 95, 106, 108, 109, 116,

Diversity 6, 38, 40, 68, 69, 82, 83, 115,

Protestant 25,
Puerto Ricans 45,
Quota(s)(immigration)
103,

Race(ism) 3, **17**, etc, etc
Refugee(s) 72, 106, 107,
Regimented(ation) 15, 35,
58, 83, 85,
Religion(ous) 66, 85,
Republican(s) 22, 25, 77,
101, 102,
Rhode Island 9,
Robinson, Bill Bogangles
87,
Roosevelt, Theodore 3
Rule of law 29, 35, 38,
Russia(n), 3, 6, 18, 37, 76,
79, 121, 122,

Santa Barbara College 11,
Science(tific) 87, 95,
Seal(s) 7, 77,
Secretary of State 7,
Secular 85,
Secular school 92,
Segregation 44,

Self-identity 32, 40, 81,
83, 84
Senate(ors) 6, 22, 76, 77,
99,
Separate(ism)(ion) 1, 6,
14, 40, 41, 57-61, 64,
73, 75, 79, 83-87, 89,
126,
Silence (as consent) 109,
Skill-based education 95,
Skilled workers 101-104,
Slave(s)(ery) 17, 19-22,
47, 67, 78, 79,
Slum 1, 49,
Social welfare 119, 120,
122,
Socialism(ist) 65, 121-
123,
Song 87,
South Korean 98,
South(erners) (USA) 23,
47,
Sports 87,
State(s) 19, 20, 92, 93,
Superior(ity) 81, 82,
Supreme Court 14, 15, 24,
45, 93,
Sweden 97,

www.ingramcontent.com/pod-product-compliance
Lightning Source LLC
Chambersburg PA
CBHW050133280326
41933CB00010B/1363